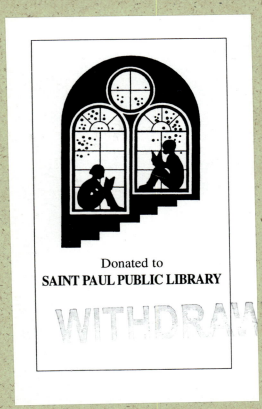

DINOSAURS
TO DODOS

DINOSAURS TO DODOS

AN ENCYCLOPEDIA OF EXTINCT ANIMALS

By Don Lessem
Illustrated by Jan Sovak

For Al Zuckerman, friend and agent extraordinaire—D.L.
For Daniela and Adrianne—J.S.

◆   ◆   ◆

Special thanks to: Ben Creisler for his expertise in nomenclature and beyond; Tess Kissinger, art coordinator; and scientific advisors Dr. Thomas Holtz, University of Maryland, Dr. Ross MacPhee, American Museum of Natural History, Dr. Andrew Noll, Harvard University, Dr. Robert Purdy, National Museum of Natural History, Dr. Nancy Simmons, American Museum of Natural History, Elizabeth Valiulis, National Museum of Natural History, and Dr. David Weishampel, Johns Hopkins University.

PHOTO CREDITS: 5: Bruce Selyem/Museum of the Rockies; 11: Reg Morrison/AUSCAPE; 15: Drumheller/Royal Tyrrell Museum; 27: John Mason/Ardea London LTD; 29: Tom McHugh/Photo Researchers; 36: Bob Cranston/Animals Animals/Earth Scenes; 62: Sinclair Stammers/Science Photo Library; 95: JM Labat/Photo Researchers

Library of Congress Cataloging-in-Publication Data
Lessem, Don. • Dinosaurs to dodos: an encyclopedia of extinct animals / by Don Lessem; art by Jan Sovak; with an introduction by Jack Horner. • p. cm. • Includes bibliographical references and index. • Summary: Presents the names, physical characteristics, and places of origin of a variety of extinct animals, arranged chronologically into eras, periods, and epochs, and discusses times of mass extinction. • ISBN 0-590-31684-2 (hardcover) • 1. Vertebrates, Fossil—Encyclopedias, Juvenile. • 2. Extinct animals—Encyclopedias, Juvenile. • [1. Prehistoric animals. 2. Vertebrates, Fossil. 3. Extinct animals. 4. Extinction (Biology)] • I. Sovak, Jan, 1953-ill. • II. Title. • QE842.L47 • 1999 • 98-25863 • 560—dc21 • CIP • AC

10 9 8 7 6 5 4 3 2 1   9/9 0/0 01 02 03

Printed in the U.S.A.   23
First edition, September 1999
Book design and composition by Nancy Sabato
Additional composition by Brad Walrod

THE BIG PICTURE

By Dr. Jack Horner

W hen my friend "Dino" Don Lessem asked me to write something for an encyclopedia of extinct animals for kids, I said sure. I think it's a neat idea. After all, as a paleontologist, I've spent most of my life studying a group of extinct animals called hadrosaurs, or duck-billed dinosaurs. Duckbills walked the Earth for several million years. But that's only a small slice of Earth's history, and it's just one group of creatures from that time.

Jack Horner excavating Tyrannosaurus Rex *in eastern Montana*

For most paleontologists, that's how work is. We study, in as much detail as we can, one particular group of animals from one period of geological time. Sometimes we look at how a group of animals lived, other times at how they were built.

And there aren't many of us looking at fossils. Fewer than one hundred scientists study dinosaurs full-time, and just a few thousand paleontologists study backboned animals from any time in the past. Others study fossil plants, or fossil insects, or other kinds of extinct life. But there aren't many of those folks, either.

Many of us paleontologists do try to look across time to see patterns in how life changes, whether suddenly by great disasters, or more slowly from changes in climate. But we don't often get a chance to think about what fossils show us of the whole history of living things on Earth. That's what I like most about this book—it shows us something of the many chapters in the story of life—from its beginning to animals that once lived alongside people.

I'll still stick to duck-billed dinosaurs as much as I can. But I think all these other animals are amazing, too. That there are many, many more creatures from the past that we haven't yet discovered is even more amazing. And, in my opinion, making new fossil discoveries is just about the most exciting thing a human being can do.

—JACK HORNER, Curator of Paleontology, Museum of the Rockies, Montana State University, Bozeman, Montana

TABLE OF CONTENTS

EXTINCTION—A WAY OF LIFE

Life is all around you. It's even in your bed, where there are hundreds of kinds of microscopic insectlike creatures called dust mites. Scientists estimate that more than 12 million distinct kinds of living things, or species, exist today—animals, plants and microorganisms.

But nearly one thousand times that number of species once lived and will never live again. They ranged in size from creatures too small to see to animals as long as three school buses. As a rule, no one species of animal lasts more than a few million years. Then its kind is replaced by another kind.

The Earth wasn't always rich with life. In fact, for nearly the first nine-tenths of the history of Earth, no creatures lived that were big enough to see without a microscope. But the Earth is so old—nearly five billion years—that it had plenty of time to make a home for an enormous variety of animals and plants.

Why have so many of these creatures gone extinct? The Earth and life keep changing. Lands and oceans shift, temperatures change. Even the air is different through time. Life must change to survive in a changing world. No one species of animal lasts forever. It goes extinct and new life-forms appear.

Sometimes the changes in the Earth are so great that enormous groups of animals and plants are wiped out in a few thousand years. That's a long time to us, but a very short time

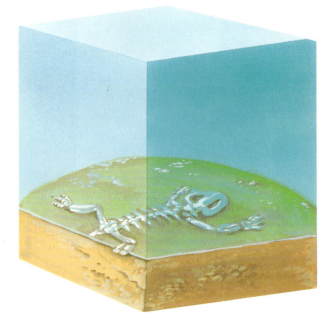
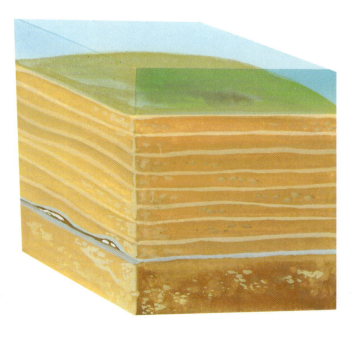

40 million years equals one inch.

by Earth history standards. These extinction "events" are the markers that scientists use to divide up the history of life.

HOW DO WE KNOW?

Fossils tell us what lived before us. Fossils are the remains and traces of ancient life. Many of these remains show us what ancient creatures looked like and where and when they lived. To figure out how prehistoric animals acted, we compare their fossils to animals alive today. We also study the marks on their fossils that can show disease or combat or accidents. And from how the fossils are distributed and from the rocks they are found in, we can sometimes tell even more. Fossils can reveal how an animal or an entire group of animals was killed, the environment of that ancient time, and when—and sometimes even how—big extinctions occurred.

HOW LIFE AND THIS BOOK ARE ORGANIZED

This book is organized as scientists organize the history of life: into eras and periods and epochs. Sometimes the end of a time unit is marked by the extinction of many kinds of animals. The book features these mass extinctions. In addition, each chapter contains a "Gallery" featuring a few of the many wonderful and long-gone creatures from that time.

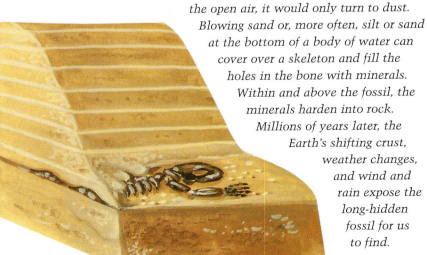

Most creatures that die aren't lucky enough to become fossils. To be preserved, a bone or other body part or a trace, such as a footprint, must be covered over quickly with sediment. Out in the open air, it would only turn to dust. Blowing sand or, more often, silt or sand at the bottom of a body of water can cover over a skeleton and fill the holes in the bone with minerals. Within and above the fossil, the minerals harden into rock. Millions of years later, the Earth's shifting crust, weather changes, and wind and rain expose the long-hidden fossil for us to find.

MOVING PLATES

The Earth's land masses are always on the move. They move too slowly for us to notice. But continents and the seafloor lie on plates that shift across the surface of the planet. These plates separate to create seas and push together to make mountains. Over just the last 600 million years of life's five-billion-year history, the land has come together to make a single continent and separated again to form the seven continents of the present-day Earth.

The Earth's lands were widely spread 600 million years ago.

Early in dinosaur times, over 200 million years ago, a single land mass called Pangaea had formed.

By the end of dinosaur times, 65 million years ago, the continents looked very much like they do today.

HOLOCENE EPOCH

TRIASSIC PERIOD   JURASSIC PERIOD   CRETACEOUS PERIOD   PALEOCENE AND EOCENE EPOCHS   OLIGOCENE, MIOCENE, AND PLIOCENE EPOCHS   PLEISTOCENE EPOCH

The Earth began as a planet without life. So how did life get started? Chemicals from within the Earth and even some from asteroids and comets that hit the Earth may have been part of the recipe. It took a long time for life on Earth to spread and develop. For billions of years, one-celled sea creatures were the only living things in the world. The oldest traces of life ever discovered are fossil bacteria over four billion years old that can be seen only under a microscope. Then, about 600 million years ago, cells began dividing and sticking together in the oceans to form far larger and more complicated life-forms.

Near the end of the Precambrian era, more complex life-forms, including the 3-to-8-inch (7.5-to-20-cm), disk-shaped Ediacaria *and the 2-to-5-inch (5-to-12.5-cm), oval-shaped* Dickinsonia, *drifted through calm, ancient seas. Without predators, their world was a peaceful one.*

40 million years equals one inch.

THE FIRST ANIMALS

On a walk in 1946, a scientist discovered some odd saucer-shaped fossils in rocks more than 600 million years old. More of these odd and very old fossils have since been found around the world. Together, they are named the Vendian animals.

At first, scientists thought the Vendian animals were the traces of ancestors of modern ocean animals such as jellyfish, soft corals, and worms. Then one scientist suggested they were "quilted" in a patterned design, without a head or rear end—unlike any modern animals. Scientists are still debating exactly what the Vendian animals were.

Lumps of cyanobacteria layered with other bacteria and minerals are found in the oceans today. They are called stromatolites. The first stromatolites (pictured above) were among the earliest life-forms nearly three billion years ago. Cyanobacteria were important to all future life on Earth. Long before plants developed, cyanobacteria used light to make oxygen. Once there was enough oxygen in the atmosphere, animals could develop.

HOLOCENE EPOCH

TRIASSIC PERIOD | JURASSIC PERIOD | CRETACEOUS PERIOD | PALEOCENE AND EOCENE EPOCHS | OLIGOCENE, MIOCENE, AND PLIOCENE EPOCHS | PLEISTOCENE EPOCH

▼ ARCHAEOSPHAEROIDES
ark-ee-oh-sfee-**roy**-dees
NAME: "ancient sphere-shaped"
TIME: over 3 billion years ago
FOSSILS FOUND: South Africa
SIZE: microscopic
Found in the same black rock as *Eobacterium*, these ball-shaped strands appear to be relatives of modern cyanobacteria.

ASPERGILLUS ▶
az-pair-**jil**-uhs
NAME: "sprinkler"
TIME: Precambrian to present
FOSSILS FOUND: Greenland
SIZE: microscopic
A kind of mold named for the shape of the spore head, which grows into a ball at the end of the long stalk.

▲ DICKINSONIA
dik-in-**soh**-nee-uh
NAME: for S. B. Dickinson, an Australian geologist
TIME: 600 million years ago
FOSSILS FOUND: Australia
SIZE: 2 to 5 inches (5 to 12.5 cm) long
Is it a worm or a different kind of animal shaped like a mattress? Scientists aren't sure from the fossil parts they've found.

CHARNIODISCUS ▶
char-nee-oh-**dis**-kuhs
NAME: "Charnwood disk," for Charnwood Forest, England
TIME: 570 million years ago
FOSSILS FOUND: Newfoundland (Canada), Europe, Australia
SIZE: 8 inches (20 cm) tall
Shaped like a feather attached to a disk, these creatures stood upright in water. They may be related to modern sea pens.

EOBACTERIUM ▶
ee-oh-bak-**tee**-ree-uhm
NAME: "dawn bacterium," because they lived at the very beginning of life on Earth
TIME: over 3 billion years ago
FOSSILS FOUND: South Africa
SIZE: microscopic
These tiny rods are among the first known bacteria-like forms.

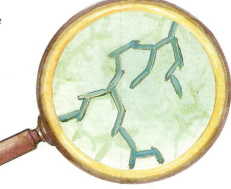

▼ KAKABEKIA

kah-kuh-**bee**-kee-uh
NAME: for Kakabeka Falls in Ontario, Canada, where it was found
TIME: 2 billion years ago
FOSSILS FOUND: Canada
SIZE: less than one-thousandth of an inch (one-hundredth of a millimeter) long
A tiny ocean creature that looked like an umbrella with a club at the end.

▲ MAWSONITES

maw-suhn-**ie**-tees
NAME: Mawson's animal, named for Sir Douglas Mawson, geologist and explorer
TIME: 580 to 570 million years ago
FOSSILS FOUND: Australia
SIZE: 5 inches (12.5 cm) across
It was probably a large circular animal made up of scaly parts and a swelling that looks like a button in the center, but scientists aren't sure. It was first thought to be a jellyfish. Some scientists think it may not be an animal at all, but a fossilized hole dug by an animal.

NOSTOC ▶

nahs-tahk
NAME: a name used by the 16th-century alchemist Paracelsus for witches' butter, a related type of modern blue-green algae
TIME: Precambrian to present
FOSSILS FOUND: worldwide
SIZE: microscopic
A kind of cyanobacteria that forms a necklace less than two-thousandths of an inch (one-fiftieth of a millimeter) long. Fossils of similar-looking bacteria have been found in Precambrian rocks around the world.

▼ SPRIGGINA

sprig-ee-nuh *or* sprih-**gie**-nuh
NAME: for R. C. Sprigg, an Australian paleontologist
TIME: 600 to 570 million years ago
FOSSILS FOUND: Australia, Africa, Russia
SIZE: 3 inches (7.5 cm) long
A wormlike animal with a crescent-shaped head. Did it stand upright on the seafloor or crawl like a worm? Nobody knows.

▲ TRIBRACHIDIUM

trie-bra-**ki**-dee-uhm
NAME: "little three arms," named for the way the animal was divided into three parts
TIME: 600 to 580 million years ago
FOSSILS FOUND: Australia
SIZE: ⅜ inch (1 cm) across
These disklike animals appear to have had tube legs like starfish, and may be very primitive relatives of sea stars.

CHAPTER 2

EARLY AND EERIE LIFE

Cambrian Period—543 million to 490 million years ago

During the Cambrian period, thousands of new creatures appeared on the ocean floor. First came animals shaped like champagne glasses and animals that lived inside tubes and hornlike structures. Then came hard-shelled grazers and the first predators. Many animals from this time seem strange to us since they have no living relatives. But others were ancestors of the worms, shelled creatures, and backboned animals of today. Increased oxygen in the oceans may have been one reason that so many new life-forms emerged at this time.

One of the first predators was Anomalocaris. It grew to 3 feet (1 m) long and had a row of spines and a circular mouth lined with 32 sharp, toothlike plates. Anomalocaris *crunched smaller creatures like trilobites or* Wiwaxia.

40 million years equals one inch.

WHICH END IS UP? THE PUZZLE OF *HALLUCIGENIA*

Its name was inspired by a word for a fantasy daydream. But for scientists, figuring out what this animal looked like has proven a nightmare. When its remains were discovered at the Burgess Shale quarry in Canada early in this century, it appeared to be a worm with bristles. Later a scientist thought it was a tube-shaped animal standing on seven pairs of stilts with tentacles on its back—and gave it the name *Hallucigenia.*

But recently, other scientists have found well-preserved relatives of *Hallucigenia* in China. These animals don't have stilt legs. What the scientist who named it thought were legs were spines along its back. The parts he thought were tentacles were fleshy legs. But which is the back and which is the front of *Hallucigenia* is still a puzzle!

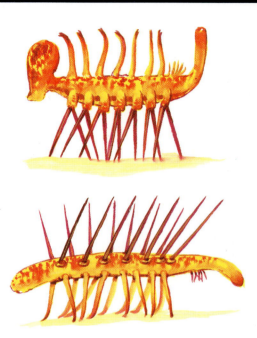

BURIED ALIVE AND *WEIRD*— THE ANIMALS OF THE BURGESS SHALE

Every once in a while, fossil-hunting scientists discover a spot where very fine grains of minerals quickly covered over whole bodies of ancient animals— preserving their soft parts as well as their shells or bones. In these rare cases, animals from millions of years ago can be seen in wonderful detail—just as they looked when they were alive.

The Burgess Shale quarry in British Columbia, Canada, is one of those magical places. More than a hundred different 530-million-year-old life-forms—some soft-bodied like jellyfish, some hard-bodied like crabs—have been discovered within the rocky layers. They were preserved when mud from a collapsing undersea shelf of coast gently covered them.

◀ ARCHAEOCYATHIDS
ahr-kee-oh-sie-**ath**-ids
NAME: "ancient cups"
TIME: 570 million to 515 million years ago
FOSSILS FOUND: Russia, South Australia, western North America
SIZE: 2 to 20 inches (5 to 50 cm) tall
Spongelike animals built like double containers, one inside the other, anchored to the seafloor.

▲ AYESHAIA
ie-**shie**-yuh
NAME: named after Ayesha Peak, in the part of British Columbia, Canada, where the fossil was found
TIME: 536 million to 518 million years ago
FOSSILS FOUND: western Canada
SIZE: ¾ inch to 1 inch (2 to 2.5 cm) long
A spiny creature with caterpillar legs, it may have punched holes in sponges to eat them.

▲ HALKIERIA
hal-**kee**-ree-uh
NAME: for Christian Halkier, conservator at the Institute for Geology in Copenhagen, Denmark
TIME: 570 million to 536 million years ago
FOSSILS FOUND: Greenland
SIZE: 2½ inches (6.25 cm) long
A sluglike animal covered with many scales.

▼ HYDROCEPHALUS
hie-droh-**sef**-uh-luhs
NAME: "water head," probably for the swollen appearance of its head
TIME: 536 million to 518 million years ago
FOSSILS FOUND: Europe, Asia, North America
SIZE: 6 inches (15 cm) long
This trilobite was very common and more widely built than others of the time.

◀ HYOLITHELLUS
hie-oh-lih-**thel**-us
NAME: "little Y fossil," for the Y-like form of the shell
TIME: 580 million to 518 million years ago
FOSSILS FOUND: Europe
SIZE: ¹/₁₀ inch (.25 cm) long
Possible early member of the mollusks, a group of animals that includes modern clams and snails. What animal lived inside the tube-shaped shell is still a mystery.

▲ KODYMIRUS

koh-di-**mie**-ruhs
NAME: "Kodym's marvel,"
for Odelon Kodym, a Czech geologist
TIME: 570 million to 536 million years ago
FOSSILS FOUND: Czech Republic
SIZE: 6 inches (15 cm) long
Perhaps the oldest member of the arthropod group ever found. Arthropods include today's crabs and many other shelled sea animals, as well as insects, spiders, centipedes, scorpions, and millipedes.

◀ LICHENOIDES ▶

lie-kin-**oi**-dees
NAME: "lichen-form," for the rough appearance of its shell plates
TIME: 536 million to 518 million years ago
FOSSILS FOUND: Europe, North Africa, USA
SIZE: 2 inches (5 cm) long
One of an extinct group of primitive animals similar to sea lilies.

◀ OLENOIDES

oh-le-**noi**-deez
NAME: "elbow-form"
TIME: 536 million to 518 million years ago
FOSSILS FOUND: worldwide
SIZE: 3 inches (7.5 cm) long
A member of a trilobite group that lasted until the time of dinosaurs, more than 300 million years later.

▲ MICRODICTYON

mie-kroh-**dik**-tee-ahn
NAME: "small net," for the netlike armored scales on its body
TIME: 536 million to 518 million years ago
FOSSILS FOUND: Canada, China
SIZE: 3 inches (7.5 cm) long
Specimens found in China in the 1980s showed that its strange plates were armor on the body of a wormlike animal with legs.

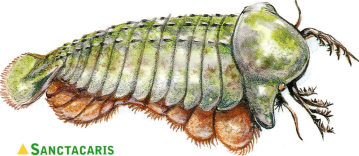

▶ PIKAIA ▶

pie-**kie**-yuh
NAME: for Pika Peak, the name of a mountain in Alberta, Canada, near the region in British Columbia where the fossil was found
TIME: 530 million years ago
FOSSILS FOUND: western Canada
SIZE: 2 inches (5 cm) long
This animal may not look very interesting, but it is important. The faint hint of a line down its back suggests it may have been an ancestor of all animals with backbones, including humans.

▲ SANCTACARIS

sank-tuh-**kair**-uhs
NAME: "saint crab," nicknamed "Santa Claws" by scientists because it had so many clawed arms around its head
TIME: 536 million to 516 million years ago
PLACE: western Canada
SIZE: 4 inches (10 cm) long
A flat-headed, wide-bodied swimmer with paddlelike gills. Unlike many Burgess Shale fossils, this animal seems to be related to many modern creatures. It could have been an ancestor of horseshoe crabs, spiders, and mites.

CHAPTER 3

A NEW UNDERWATER WORLD

Ordovician Period—490 million to 439 million years ago

S ea creatures from the Ordovician period were among the earliest ancestors of modern animals. Along the ocean bottom grew corals and ancient starfish called asterozoans. Shelled creatures on the seafloor included mollusks related to modern oysters, similar-looking brachiopods, and coiled-shell gastropods. Cephalopods, cousins of modern squid, scoured the seafloor in search of prey. But the biggest newcomers were jawless fish like *Sacabambaspis*.

Jawless fish such as Sacabambaspis, *whose fossils were found in South America, were among the first backboned animals on Earth. There were still no animals of any kind living on land.*

40 million years equals one inch.

KEEP YOUR MOUTH SHUT, FISHFACE!

Agnathans, the earliest fish, had no jaws. Their mouths were wide with strange plates on the edges of their heads. Perhaps these plates were electrical organs for sensing distance or shocking predators. Agnathans fed by sucking water containing tiny animals and sediment through their mouths. They may have swum along the sea bottoms with their tails turned upward.

SEA STRINGS

Graptolites were tiny wormlike creatures that formed colonies as coral animals do today. Entire colonies of graptolites—measuring only 2 inches (5 cm) long—drifted along the surface of the seas. They ate planktons, the same tiny sea organisms eaten in great numbers by whales today. Graptolites are especially important to scientists because they changed gradually over a long period of time. Scientists can figure out how old other sea fossils are by the kind of graptolite fossils they are found with.

Isograptus

Goniograptus

Tetragraptus

Cardiograptus

HOLOCENE EPOCH

TRIASSIC PERIOD JURASSIC PERIOD CRETACEOUS PERIOD PALEOCENE AND EOCENE EPOCHS OLIGOCENE, MIOCENE, AND PLIOCENE EPOCHS PLEISTOCENE EPOCH

THE SHELL GAME

More than 500 kinds of trilobites lived in Ordovician seas. That's not as many as in the Cambrian period, but it is still a huge number—one reason trilobite fossils are so common today.

Trilobites are easy to find not only because there were so many of them, but because they regularly shed their hard shells. The shells fell to the ancient seafloor as the animals grew, and were often covered over, becoming fossils. Thousands of different kinds of trilobites have been found in rocks made from sea bottoms around the world, from Russia to Morocco to the United States. Some had long defensive spines to ward off predators. Some had their eyes mounted on top of long stalks so they could still see while buried beneath sand and mud.

Trilobites could swim or crawl along the seafloor. But their defense against predators may have been curling their armored bodies into balls, as armadillos do today. We know trilobites were hunted by other sea creatures, since trilobite fossils are often found with bite marks in them. The rise of fish with jaws may have helped bring about the end of many trilobites. But some trilobites survived until the greatest extinction disaster of all, 251 million years ago.

A trilobite is under attack by a sea scorpion, an extinct ancestor of land scorpions. Sea scorpions belonged to a group of animals with two biting claws in front of their mouths. They were related to modern horseshoe crabs.

CONODONTS: A MYSTERY SOLVED

What are conodonts? Scientists asked this question for nearly 140 years. Conodont fossils are so tiny they have to be studied under a microscope. Most were shaped like long thin cones. Some looked like pointed rakes and combs, others like jagged bars or bumpy blades, or even plant leaves. Were they the shells of tiny animals or the teeth of slightly bigger ones? Scientists also suggested they might be parts of fish, worms, or animals with tentacles. The mystery was finally solved in 1995. Fossils from Scotland and South Africa showed that conodonts came from fishlike animals that did not have skeletons or jaws. The conodont animal was up to 2 inches (5 cm) long and looked like a little eel with bulging eyes and a fin along its tail. Each animal had many different conodonts at the bottom of its head, used for scraping or biting.

FOOD THROUGH A FILTER

Several types of shelled creatures attached themselves to the seafloor 450 million years ago. These animals filtered tiny food particles from the ocean, waving small hairs called cilia to make the water flow through their mouths. They include:

BIVALVES—*Shelled animals like clams of today, with two identical sides.*

BRACHIOPODS—*They look at first glance like bivalves, but aren't closely related. Their shells differ in size and curve. They have a beak at the hinge, and are anchored by a fleshy stalk. Brachiopods are rare now, but 500 million to 450 million years ago, they were far more common than bivalves.*

BRYOZOANS—*These tiny animals covered in lime or horn shells lived underwater in lumps or tree-shaped colonies on rocks and shells.*

SEA YOU NO MORE: THE ORDOVICIAN EXTINCTION EVENT

At the end of the Ordovician period, changing climates brought drastic changes to the world's shorelines. As the world cooled, huge glaciers formed. Sea levels dropped as the rain and snow from ocean storms fell on land and were locked in ice. Many kinds of graptolites and trilobites were among the first ocean creatures to die off from the changing weather and shrinking ocean habitats. Perhaps one in every five groups of all animals was wiped out at this time.

ARANDASPIS ▶

ayr-an-das-pis

NAME: "Aranda shield," for the aboriginal Aranda people who live in the region of Australia where fossils of this fish were found
TIME: 510 million to 463 million years ago
FOSSILS FOUND: Australia
SIZE: 5 inches (12.5 cm) long

One of the earliest known fish, it had 6 "eyes"—a pair of true eyes in the front of its head and 2 more pairs of small eyelike organs on top!

BELLEROPHON ▶

bel-air-uh-fahn

NAME: for a Greek mythical hero who rode the flying horse Pegasus
TIME: 510 million to 242 million years ago
FOSSILS FOUND: worldwide
SIZE: 3 inches (7.5 cm) long

This odd snail became extinct just before dinosaur times.

▲ BOTHRIOCIDARIS

boh-three-oh-si-dayr-uhs

NAME: "furrowed turban," for its round turbanlike shape
TIME: 510 million to 438 million years ago
FOSSILS FOUND: Europe
SIZE: ¾ inch (2 cm) across

A sea urchin relative built like a little pincushion.

CONOCARDIUM ▶

kahn-oh-kahr-dee-uhm

NAME: "conical heart," for the shape of its shell
TIME: 460 million to 254 million years ago
FOSSILS FOUND: Europe
SIZE: 2½ inches (6 cm) long

This mollusk had a shell that was fused shut, except for openings that allowed it to move, gather food, and get rid of wastes. It may have been an ancestor to modern bivalves like clams.

◀ DICHOGRAPTUS

die-koh-grap-tuhs

NAME: "two-part graptolite"
TIME: 510 million to 438 million years ago
FOSSILS FOUND: worldwide
SIZE: up to 8 inches (20 cm) long

One of the wormlike graptolites, it formed a colony of 8 branches, like the one shown here.

▲ CONSTELLARIA

kahn-stel-air-ee-uh

NAME: "star-covered animal," for the starlike bumps and pits on its surface
TIME: 510 million to 410 million years ago
FOSSILS FOUND: North America, Asia, Europe
SIZE: ⅜ inch (1 cm) tall

These branching coral-like bryozoans formed bushy colonies on the seabed.

◀ ENCRINURUS

en-kri-**noor**-uhs
NAME: "sea-lily tail," because its tail looked like another kind of animal called a crinoid, or sea lily
TIME: 439 million to 410 million years ago
FOSSILS FOUND: worldwide
SIZE: 2 inches (5 cm) long
A big-headed, bottom-living trilobite with eyes on stalks.

▼ LONCHODOMAS

lawn-koh-**doh**-mahs
NAME: "spear builder"
TIME: 470 million to 460 million years ago
FOSSILS FOUND: Europe
SIZE: 2 inches (5 cm) long
Trilobites grew spinier and stranger in this time, including this form, which had a long spike jutting forward from its head.

▲ FAVOSITELLA

fay-voh-si-**tel**-uh
NAME: "little honeycomb fossil"
TIME: 510 million to 410 million years ago
FOSSILS FOUND: North America
SIZE: microscopic
Like other bryozoans, these tiny coral-like animals formed undersea carpets made up of cuplike shells. Similar animals can be seen today on seashore rocks.

▼ ORTHOCERAS

or-**thaws**-uh-ruhs
NAME: "straight horn"
TIME: 475 million to 460 million years ago
FOSSILS FOUND: Europe
SIZE: 6 inches (15 cm) long
A cephalopod with a straight shell unlike many others of this group of mollusks.

TETRAGRAPTUS ▶

tet-ruh-**grap**-tus
NAME: "four graptolite," for its four threadlike branches
TIME: 510 million to 460 million years ago
FOSSILS FOUND: worldwide
SIZE: A branch of the colony was about 1 inch (1.5 cm) long, but each budlike animal was only about 1/25 inch (1 mm) in size
This graptolite colony with 4 branches hung downward in a cluster from a threadlike stem attached to a floating object. Tiny animals lived in the cuplike notches on the 4 branches. They fed using tentacles.

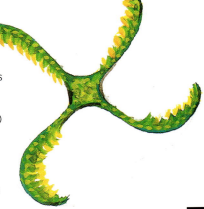

CHAPTER 4

ONTO THE LAND

Silurian and Devonian Periods—439 million to 363 million years ago

Life on land started long after ocean life. In the early Silurian period, insects and other small animals, along with plants, were the first to live on land. Wood lice crawled among small shore plants along the banks. Worms fed on rotting plants. Spiderlike predators and scorpions fed on the plant eaters. It wasn't until 40 million years later that amphibians moved from water to shoreline, where plants and plant eaters provided plenty of food. Without competition from larger animals, amphibians spread rapidly.

The earliest amphibians included Ichthyostega, *at home on land and in the water, an eel-like swamp dweller named* Greererpeton, *and* Ophiderpeton, *which likely burrowed into the mud to lie in wait for insects or to escape predators.*

40 million years equals one inch.

- ▶ **Two supercontinents form**
- ▶ **First land plants and insects develop**
- ▶ **First amphibians appear**

TEETH AND FINS

Late in the Silurian period, the first animals with both teeth and fins appeared. These "spiny sharks" were less than 6 inches (15 cm) long with streamlined bodies. They were quick hunters with big eyes and small scales.

HOW FISH GOT LEGS

Primitive amphibians like *Ichthyostega* evolved from lobe-finned fish (see p. 28). Their fishlike tail and scales show their closeness to fish. And so do their teeth, which are almost identical to lobe-finned fish teeth. But *Ichthyostega* also had features no fish ever had, including ear slits on the back of its skull.

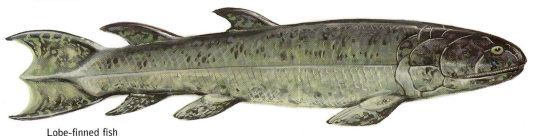

Lobe-finned fish

Ichthyostega

THE INSECTS' INVENTION

The earliest insect species are extinct. But insects are the most successful animals ever to inhabit the earth. They were the first kind of animals on land. One-third of the weight of all plant and animal life in the richest place for life, the rain forest, is made up of insects. Why have insects survived where so many others have failed?

One answer could lie in their shells. Hard skeletons protect the tiny creatures from harm and keep them from drying out when there is little rain. Insects also lay hundreds and sometimes thousands of eggs at a time. Even in the most dangerous or difficult environments, some of these eggs are likely to hatch and grow up to produce still more insects.

WEIRD NEW SWIMMERS

The bony fish of less than 450 million years ago were the likely ancestors of a new kind of predator that appeared 400 million years ago. These fish had skeletons made not of bone but of gristly cartilage. They had tiny scales. Some grew razor-sharp teeth. We call them sharks, and they have ruled the waters ever since. Sharks were just one of three new kinds of fish that emerged in the oceans of this time.

Fish with bones were also changing fast during the Silurian and Devonian periods. Among the smallest but most bony fish of all were the ray-finned fish. Half of all the kinds of living backboned animals, 20,000 species, are ray-finned fish. The stiff parallel lines of bones within their fins make their movements quick and accurate.

The third group of fish that emerged at this time were lobe-finned fish. Their fins were scaly, thick, and rounded, with heavy bones and strong muscles. Only seven kinds of fleshy lobe-finned fish survive—six kinds of lungfish and the coelacanth. Rare as they are now, lungfish or other lobe-finned fish may be the ancestors of all backboned animals that live on land. The fleshy fins evolved into legs.

The small predators shown here are an early and now extinct kind of bony fish called Cheirolepis. *The larger fish is a different kind of predator. It is an early freshwater shark, 2½ feet (75 cm) long, called* Xenacanthus.

Dunkleosteus, *a 30-foot (9-m) armored fish, chases a* Lunaspis, *another armored fish less than 1 foot (30 cm) long.*

ALMOST NO BONES ABOUT IT

Sharks are supported by cartilage skeletons, not bony ones. Only extinct jawless fish, the agnathans, had the same kind of cartilage skeletons. We have some cartilage in our bodies, including in our ears, but it cannot support weight. How did the shark cartilage get hard enough to work like bone? Tiny prism-shaped grains of limestone mix in with the outer layer of shark cartilage in a grid design. And sharks do have a little bone—a thin layer coats the outside of their cartilage skeletons.

WHY SHARKS DON'T SINK

Bony fish stay afloat with the help of a swim bladder that holds air. Sharks have no such swim bladders. What helps them float is their design. Their fins and snouts are curved on top and flat below, as airplane wings are. So moving through the water pushes them upward. Sharks must swim constantly forward—they can't stop or swim backward. However, some sharks—such as the giant whale shark— store huge amounts of light oil in their livers to help them stay afloat.

VERY MUCH ALIVE

Until fishermen netted a coelacanth in the Indian Ocean half a century ago, these primitive fish were thought to have been extinct for nearly 65 million years.

THE SKY IS FALLING: THE LATE DEVONIAN EXTINCTION EVENT

The night sky is full of fire as huge meteors crash through the sky toward the sea, 367 million years ago.

Climates grew drier and temperatures fell around the world at this time. Ocean currents swirled in new patterns, cooling the ocean further and making surface waters saltier. The oxygen content of the ocean decreased to very low levels. More weather changes may have been caused by meteorite impacts. At least three and as many as six huge objects from space may have crashed into the sea at this time. The result was the extinction of many sea creatures, including reef animals and many kinds of fish and brachiopods.

▼ CLIMATIUS

klie-**mayt**-ee-uhs
NAME: "sloping," for the sloping
spines along its back
TIME: 438 million to 390 million years ago
FOSSILS FOUND: Asia, Europe, North America
SIZE: 3 inches (7.5 cm) long
It looked like a tiny shark covered with tough
scales and had sharp spines on its belly and
back to support its fins.

FAVOSITES ▶

fay-voh-**sie**-teez
NAME: "honeycomb fossil"
TIME: 442 million to 386 million years ago
FOSSILS FOUND: Europe, USA, Southeast Asia, Australia
SIZE: about $\frac{1}{20}$ inch (1.5 mm) but formed giant colonies
5 to 6 feet (1.5 to 1.8 m) across
This ancient coral formed reefs, just as modern corals
do. Some species made large limestone domes like
modern brain coral. Other species grew in flat or
branching shapes.

▲ OONOCERAS

oh-oh-**noh**-see-ruhs
NAME: "egg horn," for the egg-shaped
pattern on its shell
TIME: 460 million to 425 million years ago
FOSSILS FOUND: Czech Republic
SIZE: 6 inches (15 cm) long
A nautoloid that swam through the sea, with
a slightly curved shell and an odd tube.

▲ PTERYGOTUS

tair-i-**goht**-uhs
NAME: "winged one," because its fossil parts looked
like wings to the quarry workers who first found it
TIME: 438 million to 411 million years ago
FOSSILS FOUND: Europe
SIZE: 5 feet (1.5 m) long
One of the largest of the Silurian eurypterids—water
predators with sharp biting claws that are related to
spiders, scorpions, and horseshoe crabs.

◀ SCYPHOCRINITES

sie-foh-krie-**nie**-teez
NAME: "cup crinoid"
TIME: 438 million to 378
million years ago
FOSSILS FOUND: Europe,
North America, Africa
SIZE: 28 inches (70 cm) high
Attached to the seafloor by
a column, this flowerlike
animal had branching arms.

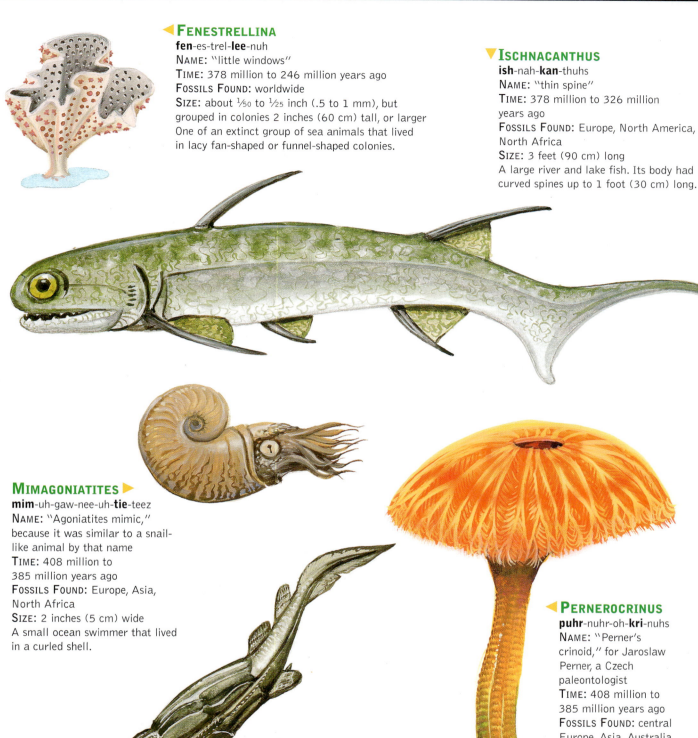

◀ FENESTRELLINA
fen-es-trel-**lee**-nuh
NAME: "little windows"
TIME: 378 million to 246 million years ago
FOSSILS FOUND: worldwide
SIZE: about 1/50 to 1/25 inch (.5 to 1 mm), but grouped in colonies 2 inches (60 cm) tall, or larger
One of an extinct group of sea animals that lived in lacy fan-shaped or funnel-shaped colonies.

▼ ISCHNACANTHUS
ish-nah-**kan**-thuhs
NAME: "thin spine"
TIME: 378 million to 326 million years ago
FOSSILS FOUND: Europe, North America, North Africa
SIZE: 3 feet (90 cm) long
A large river and lake fish. Its body had curved spines up to 1 foot (30 cm) long.

MIMAGONIATITES ▶
mim-uh-gaw-nee-uh-**tie**-teez
NAME: "Agoniatites mimic," because it was similar to a snail-like animal by that name
TIME: 408 million to 385 million years ago
FOSSILS FOUND: Europe, Asia, North Africa
SIZE: 2 inches (5 cm) wide
A small ocean swimmer that lived in a curled shell.

◀ PERNEROCRINUS
puhr-nuhr-oh-**kri**-nuhs
NAME: "Perner's crinoid," for Jaroslaw Perner, a Czech paleontologist
TIME: 408 million to 385 million years ago
FOSSILS FOUND: central Europe, Asia, Australia
SIZE: up to 18 feet (5.4 m) high and 4 feet (1.2 m) across
A huge, sunflower-like crinoid animal that lived on the edges of coral reefs.

RADOTINA ▶
rad-oh-**tee**-nah
NAME: for the town of Radotin near Prague, Czech Republic, where its fossils were found
TIME: 408 million to 385 million years ago
FOSSILS FOUND: Czech Republic
SIZE: 1 foot (30 cm) long
A small, flat-bodied and wide-finned armored fish somewhat similar to the modern ray fish.

CHAPTER 5

WET AND WILD

Carboniferous and Permian Periods—363 million to 251 million years ago

In the Carboniferous period, wet weather gave rise to strange new forests of plant life—the first forests on land. These woods were not dense and dark like today's swamp forests. They were made up of horsetail plants, thick beds of ferns, and tall, spindly trees. Strange new animals settled in this odd landscape. Amphibians of many shapes and sizes thrived in the wet. So did super-sized insects. Thick layers of fossil-rich coal are all that remain today of the great Carboniferous forests and their bizarre inhabitants.

Within a sparse 325-million-year-old swamp forest, Hylonomus, an early reptile, snaps at Meganeura, a dragonfly-like creature that was as big as a modern seagull.

40 million years equals one inch.

SCALY VEGETARIANS

Some early reptiles were the first backboned animals on land to eat plants. Amphibians were all meat eaters.

THE FIRST REPTILES

Living among the many amphibians of these forests were the first true reptiles. They looked a lot like the smaller lizardlike amphibians. But there are several important differences between amphibians and reptiles. Amphibians lay soft eggs in water. Reptiles produce eggs with hard shells, and they lay them on land. Reptiles have scaly skin rather than the moist skin of amphibians. Their kidneys and hearts are different, too, and allow them to live on dry land much more easily than amphibians can. But from fossils, it's hard to see these differences. Instead we look for other clues: The first reptiles had a smoothly curved back to their skulls. Amphibians had a deep notch in their skulls for attaching their eardrums. Reptiles also had more complicated jaw muscles, which allowed them to do more than just snap their jaws shut as amphibians do. Reptiles could bite and chew and swallow large pieces of food. We can see on fossil skulls where these jaw muscles attached.

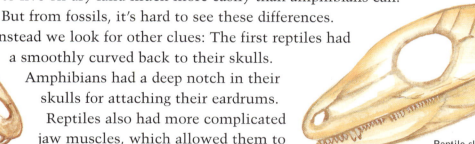

Amphibian skull

Reptile skull

Amphibians in many shapes and sometimes huge sizes were the dominant creatures in the lush, cool swamp forests more than 300 million years ago. The biggest amphibians included crocodile-like Pholidogaster *in the shallows, and the flat-bodied* Eryops, *which could grow up to 8 feet (2.4 m) long.*

TURNING OVER A NEW REEF

Huge reefs far larger than the 1,000-mile- (1,600-km-) long Great Barrier Reef of today's Australia formed 350 million years ago. One ancient reef lay along the coast of a sea that dried out, and was pushed up over time to form a Texas mountain range.

These reefs were not built by coral animals. Sponges and algae were among the animals that produced the huge mounds near the water's edge.

Other ocean animals that were doing well at this time were ammonites, brachiopods, and crinoids. Crinoids, or sea lilies, were so common in the oceans of this time that they formed undersea meadows that carpeted huge areas of the seafloor.

Some specialized sea creatures dug into the hard seafloor for food. Others grazed on food that lived on the sea bottom.

BIG AND SPINELESS

Today cephalopods live in many forms, including the largest animal in the world without a backbone—the 72-foot (22-m) giant squid.

The ocean floor was rich with life 350 million years ago. Here cephalopods search for prey among sea lilies and other seafloor organisms.

THE "HEAD-FEET" HUNTERS

Cephalopods—"head-footed" mollusks—evolved nearly 500 million years ago. By 300 million years ago, they had become big, smart, fast, and dangerous. They moved quickly backward by squirting water forward. Their jaws were equipped with sharp beaks. Ammonites (shown above) are among the most common cephalopod fossils—they grew to more than 8 feet (2.4 m) across. Their curved shells were divided into chambers, like those of their close relatives, the nautiloids of today. Ammonites vanished near the end of dinosaur times.

GOING BUGGY!

Before any plant-eating vertebrates conquered the land, insects and spiders devoured the nutrition in the plants of the Carboniferous forests. Without competition, these creepy crawlers grew to enormous size. And perhaps the air held more oxygen then, allowing them to be more active.

Whatever the cause of these good times for bugs, the results were amazing. The body alone of one spiderlike bug from Argentina, *Megarachne*, was more than 1 foot (30 cm) across! Include its huge legs, and this spider may have measured 8 feet (2.4 m) altogether. The largest flying insects were dragonfly-like creatures that could not fold their wings. They grew to more than 2 feet (60 cm) wide. Scorpions also stretched 2 feet (60 cm) across. In eastern Canada, millipede-like bugs grew longer than a person and 1 foot (30 cm) wide.

Giant bugs roamed the Carboniferous forests. Here, Megarachne, *a spiderlike creature 8 feet (2.5 cm) across, closes in on a 6-foot- (2-m-) long millipede and a scorpion 2 feet (60 cm) wide.*

BUGGING OUT

Even today most insects seem to like warm, wet environments best of all. But near the end of the Carboniferous period, the weather turned colder and drier. New plants and animals appeared, and the time of the giant insects ended.

FLY AWAY HOME

Insects were the first creatures to master flight. Reptiles, birds, mammals, and even fish have followed them into the skies.

Why did insects take to the air? To flee from predators, conquer new territories, and find new sources of food, flight was a great advantage. At first, insects may have run, jumped, or sailed down from trees. The creatures that had bodies shaped for better travel survived more often. Eventually they evolved wings. Winged insects enjoyed the greatest advantage of all—the ability to direct their safe journeys to new habitats.

THE STRANGE ROAD TO MAMMALS

Animals like *Dimetrodon* were the rulers of the land from nearly 300 million years ago until shortly before the rise of the dinosaurs in the Triassic period—more than 70 million years later.

They belonged to a group of backboned land animals called synapsids—"together arches"—named for the single opening on each side of their skulls. Some were plant eaters, but most were vicious meat eaters with powerful jaws and steak-knife-style teeth. Though they evolved from animals less than 2 feet (60 cm) long, synapsids soon produced species 10 feet (3 m) long and weighing 450 pounds (200 kg). They replaced most of the earlier large reptiles of 300 million years ago, the anapsids ("no arches"), such as the plant-eating pareiasaurs. The hippopotamus-sized pareiasaurs were clumsy and slow-moving, the ancestors of turtles. They were no match for the synapsids.

> ## NOT A DINOSAUR
>
> *Dimetrodon* is often grouped with dinosaurs. That's a big mistake. *Dimetrodon* lived long before any dinosaur and was more closely related to *us* than to dinosaurs.

A 9-foot- (2.7-m-) long predator, Dimetrodon, *chases an equally large plant eater,* Diadectes. *These creatures were the dominant land animals of their time, 280 million years ago.*

SAILING AWAY

Sails of skin over backbones are a feature of several land animals. *Dimetrodon* and other 280-million-year-old synapsids had them. So did some dinosaurs. Even some modern lizards have sails. Long ago scientists guessed that the sails helped these animals navigate across water. Then other scientists suggested that sails were displays to frighten rivals and impress mates.

Now scientists think the sails had another purpose. Plenty of blood passed through the skin and bone of *Dimetrodon*'s sail. In the morning sun, the sail might have been a solar panel for passing the sun's warmth right into its blood.

Heating up from its sail, *Dimetrodon* could get moving earlier than other cold-blooded animals, which also relied on the warmth of their environment for energy but could not heat up as quickly.

THE HOLE STORY

Scientists group many land animals—including birds, reptiles, and mammals—in part by the number of holes in their heads:

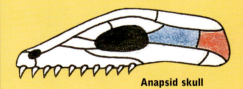

Anapsid skull

ANAPSIDS *are animals with no windows in their skulls. The first fossil reptiles were anapsids and so are turtles and tortoises.*

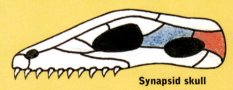

Synapsid skull

SYNAPSIDS *have a single hole, placed low on each side of their skulls. Sail-backed Dimetrodon was a synapsid, and so are we and other mammals.*

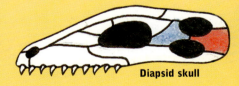

Diapsid skull

DIAPSIDS *have two openings at the back of their skulls. Crocodiles, lizards, dinosaurs, pterosaurs, and birds all have two skull holes on each side of their heads.*

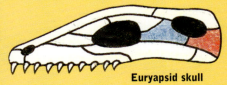

Euryapsid skull

EURYAPSIDS *were diapsids, but they had just a single hole high on the side of their skulls. They included the giant swimming reptiles of dinosaur times, such as* Plesiosaurus.

ALMOST THE END: THE PERMIAN EXTINCTION EVENT

A huge mountain explodes with lava and hot gases, actually cooking the nearby ocean life. This is just one of the possible disasters that might have occurred 245 million years ago.

At the time of "The Great Dying," life came closer to disappearing *entirely* than at any time before or since. More than nine in ten of all sea creatures were wiped out, and so were many animals on land. Changes in the movements of the world's water brought poisonous carbon dioxide and methane gas up from the seafloor. Erupting volcanoes also brought more carbon dioxide into the water. Seas rose and then fell, destroying the habitats of many shoreline animals. Trilobites disappeared entirely in this extinction. On land, many kinds of insects and amphibians were wiped out.

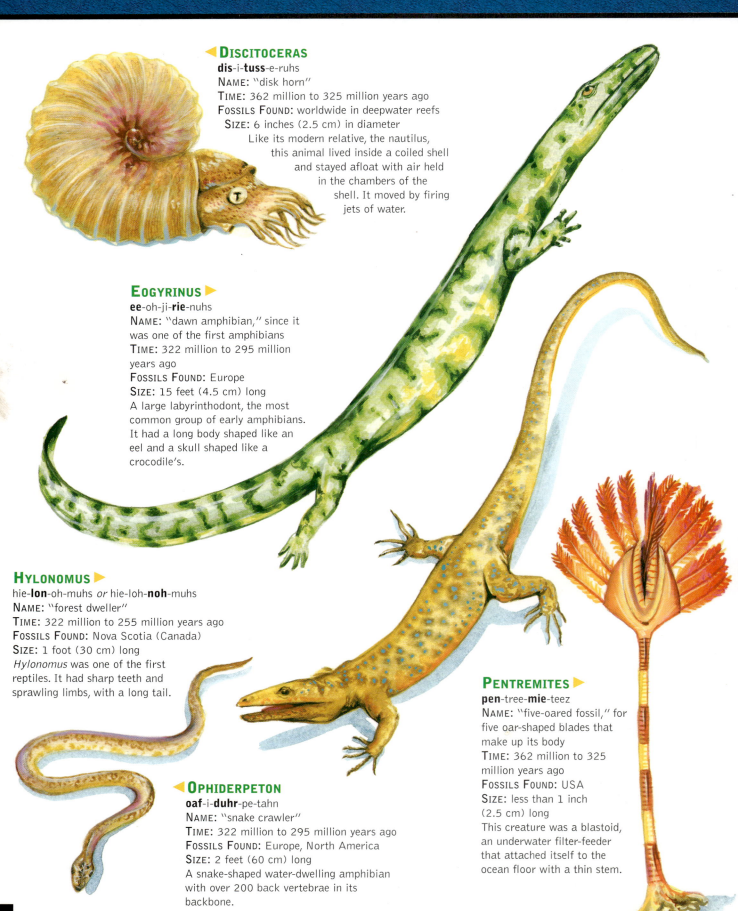

◀ DISCITOCERAS
dis-i-**tuss**-e-ruhs
NAME: "disk horn"
TIME: 362 million to 325 million years ago
FOSSILS FOUND: worldwide in deepwater reefs
SIZE: 6 inches (2.5 cm) in diameter
Like its modern relative, the nautilus, this animal lived inside a coiled shell and stayed afloat with air held in the chambers of the shell. It moved by firing jets of water.

EOGYRINUS ▶
ee-oh-ji-**rie**-nuhs
NAME: "dawn amphibian," since it was one of the first amphibians
TIME: 322 million to 295 million years ago
FOSSILS FOUND: Europe
SIZE: 15 feet (4.5 cm) long
A large labyrinthodont, the most common group of early amphibians. It had a long body shaped like an eel and a skull shaped like a crocodile's.

HYLONOMUS ▶
hie-**lon**-oh-muhs or hie-loh-**noh**-muhs
NAME: "forest dweller"
TIME: 322 million to 255 million years ago
FOSSILS FOUND: Nova Scotia (Canada)
SIZE: 1 foot (30 cm) long
Hylonomus was one of the first reptiles. It had sharp teeth and sprawling limbs, with a long tail.

◀ OPHIDERPETON
oaf-i-**duhr**-pe-tahn
NAME: "snake crawler"
TIME: 322 million to 295 million years ago
FOSSILS FOUND: Europe, North America
SIZE: 2 feet (60 cm) long
A snake-shaped water-dwelling amphibian with over 200 back vertebrae in its backbone.

PENTREMITES ▶
pen-tree-**mie**-teez
NAME: "five-oared fossil," for five oar-shaped blades that make up its body
TIME: 362 million to 325 million years ago
FOSSILS FOUND: USA
SIZE: less than 1 inch (2.5 cm) long
This creature was a blastoid, an underwater filter-feeder that attached itself to the ocean floor with a thin stem.

COELUROSAURAVUS ▼

see-lor-oh-**sor**-uh-vuhs
NAME: "coelurosaur ancestor," because it was wrongly thought to be an ancestor of small meat-eating dinosaurs
TIME: 260 million to 246 million years ago
FOSSILS FOUND: Madagascar
SIZE: 1 foot (30 cm) wingspan
The earliest known gliding reptile.

COLLEMATARIA ▶

kohl-eh-ma-**tair**-ee-uh
NAME: "cemented shell," for the way its 2 shells fit closely together
TIME: 280 million to 243 million years ago
FOSSILS FOUND: Texas (USA)
SIZE: 2 inches (5 cm) across
This brachiopod had an odd shape with flutelike ribs from spine-shaped supports.

ELGINIA ▶

el-**jin**-ee-uh
NAME: for Elgin, Scotland, where it was found
TIME: 260 million to 246 million years ago
FOSSILS FOUND: Europe
SIZE: 2 feet (.6 m) long
This plant eater was an anapsid, one of the early reptiles without skull holes. It was one of the smaller of the pareiasaurs, ancestors of turtles.

ERYOPS ▶

er-ee-ahps
NAME: "drawn-out face"
TIME: 300 million to 260 million years ago
FOSSILS FOUND: Texas (USA)
SIZE: 5 feet (1.5 m) long
Eryops was one of the largest groups of early amphibians, the temnospondyls. It was heavy, had a big skull, and may have lived on land and in the water.

◀ MESOSAURUS

me-soh-**sor**-uhs
NAME: "intermediate lizard," because it seemed to be related to many types of reptiles
TIME: 280 million to 260 million years ago
FOSSILS FOUND: Brazil, South Africa
SIZE: over 2 feet (60 cm) long
A primitive swimming reptile with a long tail and paddle arms.

CHAPTER 6

THE RISE OF REPTILES

Triassic Period—251 million to 208 million years ago

The Triassic period was a time of great change all around the planet. Pterosaurs, the flying reptiles, first took to the air, and giant reptiles first swam the seas. On land, reptiles—including big meat eaters, lightly built hunters, armored plant eaters with piglike snouts, and crocodile-like fish eaters—lived alongside the first dinosaurs. Many reptiles were larger and more common than the first dinosaurs. But both reptiles and dinosaurs were much bigger than the first mammals. The mammals that emerged at this time grew no bigger than mice.

Ox-sized Kannemeyeria *rips up roots and leaves.* Lystrosaurus, *as big as a pig, snaps up weeds. Another* Lystrosaurus *wallows nearby. Its nostrils were placed so far back on its skull that it could breathe with only the top of its head above the waterline.*

40 million years equals one inch.

▶ Giant reptiles rule the land
▶ First dinosaurs develop
▶ Flying reptiles take to the skies

THE HOLE WORLD OF DICYNODONTS

The Triassic period featured plant eaters that chewed like no animals before or since. Large dicynodonts chomped worldwide in warm, wet climates on the single supercontinent of the time. Their name means "two dog-teeth." Their upper jaws ended in a beak. Two tusks, like a dog's sharp canine teeth, emerged from this beak. Powered by strong jaw muscles, the tusks sliced against a notch in the lower jaws to cut tough plants.

Some dicynodonts may have used their strong snouts to build underground homes. *Cistecephalus* had a wedge-shaped snout ideal for digging. And in South Africa, spiral-shaped burrows from the Triassic period have been discovered. Inside, scientists found dicynodont bones and eggs.

Cistecephalus sits on its eggs.

While dicynodonts were the most common plant eaters of their time, some were also insect eaters. Little Ericiolacerta, just 8 inches (20 cm) long, had long legs for chasing bugs and small teeth for biting them.

HOLOCENE EPOCH

TRIASSIC PERIOD   JURASSIC PERIOD   CRETACEOUS PERIOD   PALEOCENE AND EOCENE EPOCHS   OLIGOCENE, MIOCENE, AND PLIOCENE EPOCHS   PLEISTOCENE EPOCH

KILLERS BEFORE DINOSAURS

Before and alongside the dinosaurs lived many other kinds of meat eaters that did not survive the Triassic period. The largest grew to twice the weight of any Triassic dinosaur. These giant early reptiles were the last of the thecodonts, four-legged early reptiles that were the ancestors of crocodiles and dinosaurs. During the Triassic period, thecodonts grew more lightly built and more able to walk like dinosaurs did, with their legs held underneath their bodies.

But the most successful of all relatives of early reptiles were the cynodonts. Most were meat eaters, and few grew bigger than 3 feet (90 cm) long. They had much in common with mammals. Both cynodonts and mammals could breathe while they chewed. They both had several different kinds of teeth. Cynodonts had whiskers, and perhaps body hair, as mammals do. Cynodonts also could run fast with their legs held underneath their bodies. Perhaps cynodonts were even warm-blooded.

Erythrosuchus is on the hunt in the warm Triassic landscape. This 15-foot- (4.5-m-) long thecodont reptile was far more powerful but not nearly as quick as Thrinaxodon, its cynodont prey.

Lagosuchus was a rabbit-sized meat eater that may have been an ancestor of dinosaurs.

UP ON TWO LEGS

Late in the Triassic period, new kinds of little meat-eating reptiles appeared. With long tails and short bodies, they were able to run on their hind legs. These animals included lizard eaters just 1 foot (30 cm) long that may have been ancestors to dinosaurs, and small insect catchers that may have lived in trees and been the ancestors of flying reptiles.

YOU'LL KNOW BY THE NOSE

How do you tell a phytosaur from a crocodile? One easy way is to look up their noses. Phytosaurs had nostrils nearly even with their eyes. Crocodile nostrils are placed near the tips of their snouts. Don't worry about finding these creatures side by side, though. Phytosaurs have been extinct for 200 million years.

UP, UP, AND AWAY—THE PTEROSAURS

Long before birds or bats, the first backboned animals to fly were reptiles. We call them pterosaurs, and they took wing in the Triassic period. Some were no bigger than robins. Others were giants as wide as jet fighter planes—the largest animals ever in the air. The first pterosaurs were less than 6 feet (1.8 m) wide, with teeth and tails. They belonged to a group called rhamphornychoids, and they lived near seas around the world.

Much later, toward the end of dinosaur time, pterosaurs evolved that had no teeth or tails. Some grew so large—over 40 feet (12 m) wide—that scientists think they must have been gliders with little flying skill.

Eudimorphodon, an early pterosaur, was smaller than crows are today. But this reptile was an agile flier. It probably scooped fish from the water as a pelican does.

Most pterosaurs were fish eaters that sailed low over the water and snapped up fish with their narrow jaws. A few developed more specialized feeding habits. One pterosaur we know, *Pterodaustro*, even had a comb in its mouth. Straining water through this sieve, the pterosaur could sift out tiny living things to eat, as many whales do today.

Like birds, pterosaurs had hollow bones and large brains. And like birds they could see far but not smell well. But pterosaurs had no feathers. They had leathery skin and fur, and wings that grew from their enormously long fourth fingers. Their first three fingers may have worked as hooks to help them roost on tree branches or cliffs.

FLYING REPTILE FACE

Pterosaurs varied enormously in wingspan, from as small as robins to as large as fighter planes. But what sets the many kinds of pterosaurs apart even more than size are the shapes of their teeth and skulls.

Anurognathus *was a small pterosaur, one of a group of agile, short-tailed fliers that appeared in the late Jurassic period. Its small teeth suggest that it may have caught insects, not fish, using its flying skill.*

Dsungaripterus *was a Chinese pterosaur from the Cretaceous period. This mid-sized flying reptile grew to nearly 10 feet (3 m) long. No one knows what its unusual head crest was for.*

Pterodaustro, *from Argentina, had a very strange, long mouth. Its lower teeth were shaped like small bristles. This pterosaur may have scooped up water in its jaws and strained it through the bristles to capture tiny animals.*

Quetzalcoatlus *had an enormous, toothless skull on a body with a wingspan of 40 feet (12 m)! This giant may have dived into the water to catch fish in its jaws as a pelican does. Its crest may have helped keep it stable in flight.*

Tropeognathus *was a Cretaceous pterosaur that ranged over South America. It had odd crests on both the front and back of its skull and a 20-foot (6-m) wingspan.*

REPTILE MONSTERS IN THE SEA

Reptiles invaded the water 235 million years ago, in the middle of the Triassic period. They grew to enormous size—as large as whales—and ruled the seas until the end of dinosaur time, 170 million years later. The first large ocean reptiles were nothosaurs. They had long, spiky teeth for catching fish and webbed toes to help them paddle. Placodonts lived at the same time. These sea reptiles were 6 feet (1.8 m) long with armored sides. Placodonts crushed and ate shellfish on the seafloor using huge, flat teeth on the roofs of their mouths and along the edges of their jaws.

By 200 million years ago, plesiosaurs had appeared. These sea reptiles had short tails and broad paddle arms, and most had very long necks. At 40 feet (12 m) long, the short-necked pliosaurs were the biggest plesiosaurs of all, longer than moving vans. Ichthyosaurs, which also appeared at this time, grew even bigger—50 feet (15 m) long. They mysteriously disappeared 90 million years ago. But fierce fish-eating sea reptiles just as big—mosasaurs—lasted to the end of dinosaur time, 65 million years ago.

A long-necked plesiosaur snatches a fish in its jaws near the surface of the water.

UNDERWATER UGLIES

Plagiosaurs were odd, armored amphibians that lived in Europe during the Triassic period. They breathed through feathery gills and waited for prey on the bottom of ponds, lakes, and rivers. The weird *Gerrothorax* was a 3-foot- (1-m-) long plagiosaur. Its body and head were wide and flat, and it had body armor and tiny limbs.

Much bigger amphibians called capitosaurs may have hunted plagiosaurs. *Cyclotosaurus* was as long as a crocodile but had small legs that could barely support its body out of water.

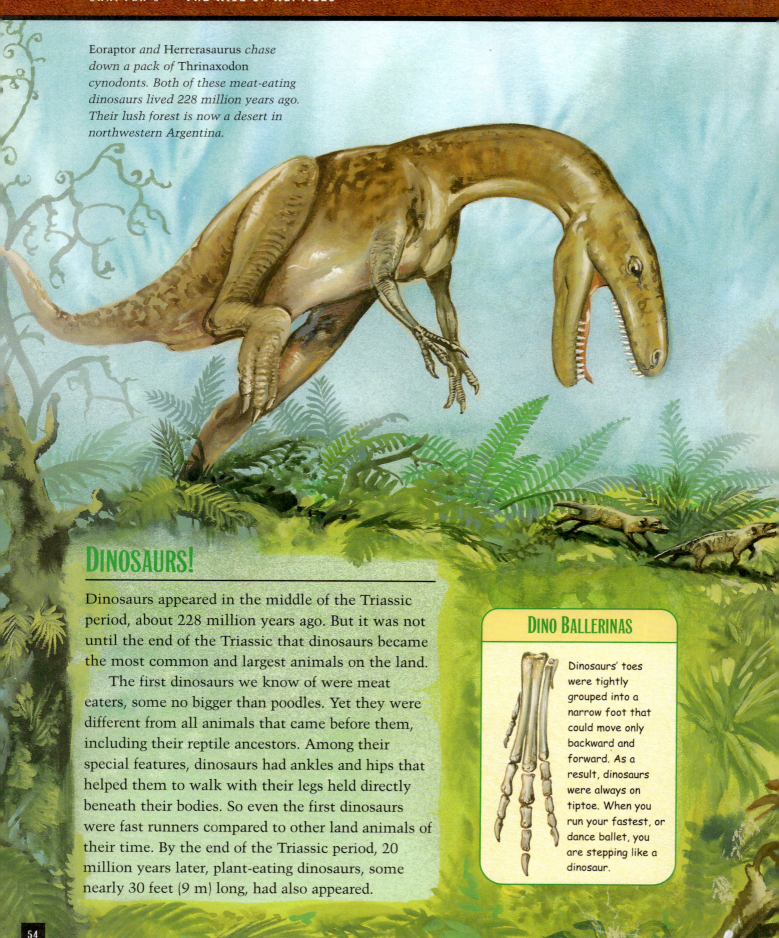

Eoraptor and *Herrerasaurus chase down a pack of* Thrinaxodon *cynodonts. Both of these meat-eating dinosaurs lived 228 million years ago. Their lush forest is now a desert in northwestern Argentina.*

DINOSAURS!

Dinosaurs appeared in the middle of the Triassic period, about 228 million years ago. But it was not until the end of the Triassic that dinosaurs became the most common and largest animals on the land.

The first dinosaurs we know of were meat eaters, some no bigger than poodles. Yet they were different from all animals that came before them, including their reptile ancestors. Among their special features, dinosaurs had ankles and hips that helped them to walk with their legs held directly beneath their bodies. So even the first dinosaurs were fast runners compared to other land animals of their time. By the end of the Triassic period, 20 million years later, plant-eating dinosaurs, some nearly 30 feet (9 m) long, had also appeared.

DINO BALLERINAS

Dinosaurs' toes were tightly grouped into a narrow foot that could move only backward and forward. As a result, dinosaurs were always on tiptoe. When you run your fastest, or dance ballet, you are stepping like a dinosaur.

CANNIBALS?

Early dinosaurs did not simply hunt other animals. Sometimes they were cannibals. In the American Southwest, scientists have found skeletons of dozens of *Coelophysis*, a small meat-eating dinosaur. In the stomach cavity of the adults may be the bones of youngsters of the same kind of dinosaur. *Coelophysis* may have been eating the young of its own kind.

LUCKY DINOSAURS, UNLUCKY REPTILES: LATE TRIASSIC EXTINCTION EVENT

We think of the end of the dinosaurs 65 million years ago as one of the world's greatest extinctions. But more kinds of animals were wiped out as the dinosaurs rose to dominate the land 200 million years ago. In the ocean many kinds of ammonites, bivalves, and conodonts died out. On land, many early relatives of reptiles, large amphibians, and plants were destroyed, while dinosaurs survived.

A rapid drop in sea level may have killed off many of the animals. Not only would a drop in sea level change ocean conditions, it could have caused more extreme seasons on land. But why did the seas fall? Maybe the slow splitting of the world's one continent along what would later become the Atlantic Ocean caused the drop in ocean levels.

▼ AEGER

ee-guhr
NAME: for the sea god called Aegir in Scandinavian mythology
TIME: 210 to 150 million years ago
FOSSILS FOUND: worldwide
SIZE: 4¾ inches (12 cm) long
This long-tailed crustacean looked like a modern shrimp. It had 10 legs and long antennae.

▲ CYMBOSPONDYLUS

sim-boh-**spohn**-dil-uhs
NAME: "cup vertebra," for the hollowed out, cuplike shape of its vertebrae
TIME: 240 million to 235 million years ago
FOSSILS FOUND: North America
SIZE: 32 feet (9.6 m) long
One of the early ichthyosaurs ("fish lizards"), a group which lived in shallow seas for 130 million years. Many ichthyosaurs later grew to look more like dolphins.

◀ EUPARKERIA

yoo-pahr-**keer**-ee-uh
NAME: for W. K. Parker, a British scientist
TIME: 235 million years ago
FOSSILS FOUND: South Africa
SIZE: 2 feet (60 cm) long
A socket-toothed reptile, or thecodont. The thecodonts were ancestors of crocodiles, dinosaurs, and pterosaurs. It was small and lightly built compared to other thecodonts.

▼ EORAPTOR

ee-oh-**rap**-tuhr
NAME: "dawn thief"
TIME: 228 million years ago
FOSSILS FOUND: South America
SIZE: 4 feet (1.2 m) long
One of the first dinosaurs, a dog-sized meat eater only recently discovered.

◀ HYPSOGNATHUS

hip-sawg-**nay**-thus *or*
hip-**sawg**-nuh-thuhs
NAME: "deep jaw," for the shape of its lower jaw
TIME: 220 million to 208 million years ago
FOSSILS FOUND: New Jersey (USA)
SIZE: 1 foot (30 cm) long
One of the last of a group of early anapsid reptiles, the procolophonids. It was smaller than most procolophonids, but like them it had thick, sprawling limbs and a thick skull.

LONGISQUAMA ▶

lawn-gee-skwah-mah
NAME: "long scales"
TIME: 240 million years ago
FOSSILS FOUND: central Asia
SIZE: 6 inches (15 cm) long
A lizardlike thecodont, it had tall scales on its back. It may have used these scales for gliding.

▲ MASSETOGNATHUS

ma-**see**-tag-**nay**-thuhs
NAME: "chewing jaw"
TIME: 230 million years ago
FOSSILS FOUND: South America
SIZE: 19 inches (47.5 cm) long
One of the few plant eaters among the cynodonts, which were ancestors of modern mammals. It had teeth and jaws like a beaver's, designed for nipping and chewing plants.

▶ NOTHOSAURUS

noh-thoh-**sor**-uhs
NAME: "mongrel lizard," because the scientist who named it thought it looked like a cross between a *Plesiosaurus* and a crocodile
TIME: 225 million to 210 million years ago
FOSSILS FOUND: Germany
SIZE: 10 feet (3 m) long
Nothosaurs were among the first large marine reptiles. They had sharp teeth for catching fish.

PLATEOSAURUS ▶

playt-ee-oh-**sor**-uhs
NAME: "broad lizard," for its large and strong limb bones
TIME: 208 million years ago
FOSSILS FOUND: western Europe
SIZE: 26 feet (9.4 m) long
One of the first prosauropods, plant-eating dinosaurs with long necks, little heads, and five-fingered hands. Perhaps they reared up on their long back legs to feed on tree branches.

TANYSTROPHEUS ▶

tan-ee-**stroh**-fee-uhs
NAME: "stretched vertebrae"
TIME: 220 million years ago
FOSSILS FOUND: central Europe, the Middle East
SIZE: up to 20 feet (6 m) long
This fishing reptile had an extremely long neck. It lived on land while young, and in the sea as an adult.

CHAPTER 7

DINOSAUR GIANTS
Jurassic Period—208 million to 146 million years ago

D inosaurs dominated the land during the Jurassic period. Over 55 million years, dinosaurs developed into plant eaters and meat eaters as small as chickens and as big as buildings. Meanwhile, the planet's single land was dividing into two huge continents. Plants and climates were becoming more varied. But the earth was still warm and without grass or flowers.

We know from fossil footprints that giant plant-eating dinosaurs like these 70-foot (21-m) Camarasaurus sheltered their young in the center of the herd.

40 million years equals one inch.

MUNCHING MONSTERS

The biggest animals yet to walk the Earth appeared at this time: the sauropods. These four-legged plant eaters had tiny heads and enormous bodies. They nipped plants with spoon-shaped or pencil-shaped teeth and digested them in their huge guts with help from rocks they swallowed.

The sauropods evolved from prosauropods, dinosaurs nearly 30 feet (9 m) long that first appeared in the Triassic period. The sauropods split into many groups, which varied in size and appearance. The diplodocids, with their whiplike tails, were the longest of all. *Seismosaurus* was a diplodocid more than 120 feet (36 m) long. That's the length of four school buses!

But the biggest of all Jurassic sauropods were the brachiosaurids, with high giraffelike chests and broad bodies. Some brachiosaurs were six stories high and weighed as much as 50 elephants. Big as they were, these animals still might have been hunted by giant meat eaters like *Allosauru*s, which grew to nearly 40 feet (12 m) long.

WHALE OF A DINOSAUR

Sir Richard Owen, the man who made up the name "dinosaur" ("frighteningly big lizard"), also was the first to name a sauropod dinosaur. A backbone from a giant sauropod had been found and was thought to be a whale's bone. But Owen thought the backbone belonged to a whale-sized crocodile, and he called it *Cetiosaurus*, or "whale lizard."

Owen's *Cetiosaurus*

Bird-hipped
Stegosaurus

Lizard-hipped
Allosaurus

GETTING HIP: BIRD-HIPS VS. LIZARD-HIPS

Dinosaurs evolved in two very different groups, according to how their hips were built. Lizard-hips, or saurischians, had a pubic bone in their hips that pointed down. Lizard-hips included the giant sauropod plant eaters and all the meat-eating dinosaurs, the theropods.

Ornithischians, the bird-hipped dinosaurs, had a pubic bone that pointed backward. Bird-hipped dinosaurs ranged from little hypsilophodontids to familiar big plant eaters such as *Stegosaurus*, and included horned dinosaurs and duckbills in the next dinosaur period—the Cretaceous.

HOLOCENE EPOCH

TRIASSIC PERIOD   JURASSIC PERIOD   CRETACEOUS PERIOD   PALEOCENE AND EOCENE EPOCHS   OLIGOCENE, MIOCENE, AND PLIOCENE EPOCHS   PLEISTOCENE EPOCH

×20

FOR THE BIRDS

In Germany there is a mine where limestone 145 million years old perfectly preserves animals that died in or near an ancient lagoon with poisonous waters. Among the many beautiful fossils found in this stone quarry are eight fossils of a 1-foot- (30-cm-) long bird. It is the oldest bird ever found. Its name is *Archaeopteryx* ("ancient feathered wing").

This long-extinct animal was different from nearly all modern birds. It had teeth, claws on its wings, and a long bony tail. These are features of dinosaurs and other reptiles. But it also had feathers like a bird. Except for feathers, it looked so much like a small meat-eating dinosaur that one *Archaeopteryx* was thought to be a dinosaur until its faint feather impressions were spotted in the rock around its skeleton.

Bird fossils from dinosaur times remain rare, but *Archaeopteryx* shows so many features of a meat-eating dinosaur that most scientists think it evolved from dinosaurs.

LOST TREASURE

Archaeopteryx is one of the most treasured fossils in the world. Only eight are known, and their value to science is beyond measuring. If sold, they might bring millions of dollars. One *Archaeopteryx* was stolen in the 1980s and is still missing.

Archaeopteryx flies over a lagoon amid Rhamphorhynchus *pterosaurs. Below, the little dinosaur* Compsognathus *runs along the shore chasing a small mammal.*

DINOSAURS WITH FEATHERS

New discoveries from China show little meat-eating dinosaurs with what appear to be quills or feathers. These dinosaurs lived after *Archaeopteryx* in the next dinosaur period, the Cretaceous. They were not fliers. What does this mean? Perhaps some meat-eating dinosaurs had something like feathers meant to help them keep warm, not to fly. And, confusing as it sounds, lizard-hipped dinosaurs, not bird-hipped dinosaurs, are the ancestors of modern birds.

◀ ALLOSAURUS
al-oh-**sor**-uhs
NAME: "strange lizard," for the unusual way its backbones were shaped to make them lighter
TIME: 155 million to 145 million years ago
FOSSILS FOUND: western North America
SIZE: up to 40 feet (12 m) long
The largest Jurassic predator, with strong, 3-fingered hands and powerful jaws.

APATOSAURUS ▶
uh-**pat**-oh-**sor**-uhs
NAME: "deceptive lizard"
TIME: 145 million years ago
FOSSILS FOUND: western North America
SIZE: up to 90 feet (27 m) long
This huge plant-eating dinosaur is commonly but mistakenly called "Brontosaurus." A famous paleontologist had given it 2 different names: *Apatosaurus* and *Brontosaurus*. When scientists figured out that both were the same animal, they decided that the first name given, *Apatosaurus*, should be used.

◀ DILOPHOSAURUS
die-**loh**-fuh-**sor**-uhs
NAME: "two-crested lizard"
TIME: 200 million to 190 million years ago
FOSSILS FOUND: Arizona, China
SIZE: 20 feet (6 m) long
One of the first large meat-eating dinosaurs in the early Jurassic. It did not spit poison as it was shown doing in the film *Jurassic Park*.

▼ DIMORPHODON
die-**mor**-foh-dahn
NAME: "two form tooth," for its 2 kinds of teeth—long stabbing teeth in the front and smaller pointed teeth along the back of its jaws
TIME: 150 million years ago
FOSSILS FOUND: England, Mexico
SIZE: 5 feet (1.5 m) wide in wingspan
Dimorphodon was a rhamphorhynchoid pterosaur with the long tail typical of that group of flying reptiles. It had a large head with biting teeth.

▲ LEPTOLEPIS
lep-toh-lep-is
NAME: "thin scale"
TIME: 200 million to 145 million years ago
FOSSILS FOUND: worldwide
SIZE: 9 inches (22.5 cm) long
It was shaped like a herring. Its jaws opened wide, and its scales were thinner than those of earlier bony fish.

◀ MAMENCHISAURUS

ma-**men**-chee-**sor**-uhs
NAME: "Mamenchi reptile,"
for the Mamenchi Ferry on
the Upper Chang Jiang River
in Sichuan Province, China
TIME: 150 million years ago
FOSSILS FOUND: Asia
SIZE: 65 feet to 90 feet
(19.5 m to 27 m) long
The longest necked animal
that ever lived—its neck was
33 feet (10 m) long!

▼ METRIORHYNCHUS

met-ree-oh-**rin**-kuhs
NAME: "medium snout," because its
snout was shorter than that of some
other marine crocodiles
TIME: 160 million to 146 million
years ago
FOSSILS FOUND: Europe, South America
SIZE: 10 feet (3 m) long
This water-living crocodile had no
armor. Its legs were paddles, and its
tail was shaped like a
fish's fin to help
it swim.

▼ MONOLOPHOSAURUS

mon-oh-loh-foh-**sor**-uhs
NAME: "single-crested reptile"
TIME: 165 million years ago
FOSSILS FOUND: China
SIZE: 20 feet (6 m) long
A large and recently discovered
meat eater with a crest.

▼ RHOMALEOSAURUS

roh-**may**-lee-oh-**sor**-uhs
NAME: "strong lizard"
TIME: 175 million years ago
FOSSILS FOUND: Europe
SIZE: 11 feet to 25 feet (4 m
to 8 m) long
One of the first short-necked
plesiosaurs. It was much
smaller than later
members of this
giant sea reptile
group, with a
neck ¼ the
length of its
body.

TUOJIANGOSAURUS ▶

twaw-**jyawng**-oh-**sor**-uhs
NAME: "Tuo Jiang lizard,"
for the Tuo Jiang River in
Sichuan Province, China
TIME: 150 million years ago
FOSSILS FOUND: China
SIZE: 20 feet (6 m) long
One of the earlier stegosaurs, this
plant eater had plates on its back that
were shaped like spikes.

CHAPTER 8

THE GREAT DINOSAUR PERIOD

Cretaceous Period—146 million to 65 million years ago

The Cretaceous period was the last dinosaur period, a time of great change in the look of the earth. Continents took on shapes very much like those of today, after seas reached record heights. Flowers appeared, and so did many insects from bees to ants. Giant lizards swam in the oceans, along with huge turtles. In the skies, pterosaurs stretched to 40 feet (12 m) in wingspan. On land, the dinosaurs ruled in sizes and shapes beyond any seen before. Plant eaters grew to 100 tons, and meat eaters reached over 40 feet (12 m) in length.

Duck-billed dinosaurs, or hadrosaurs, were the most advanced plant eaters ever. And duckbills such as this Maiasaura may have been caring parents, feeding their helpless young in the nest.

40 million years equals one inch.

► Biggest dinosaurs ever walk the land
► First primates develop
► First flowers appear

CARNIVORE KINGS

New forms of giant meat eaters emerged in the Cretaceous period. All had powerful jaws with short front legs and long back legs. The last of the killer giants was the smartest and most powerful—*Tyrannosaurus rex*. But 35 million years earlier, even bigger killers lived in North Africa and South America.

The biggest meat eater of all was *Giganotosaurus*. This dinosaur from Argentina was over 40 feet (12 m) long and weighed up to 10 tons. That's at least a station wagon heavier than the biggest *T. rex*.

And while *T. rex* was one of the biggest of all the animals in *its* world, *Giganotosaurus* ate plant eaters many times its own size. The largest animal ever to walk the Earth lived in the same place and near the same time as *Giganotosaurus*. It was the 100-ton plant eater *Argentinosaurus*.

SLICE AND DICE

Giganotosaurus's sharp, thin teeth were ideal for slicing. They had sharp serrations like a steak knife. *T. rex* teeth were serrated also, but were much thicker, for breaking through bones or holding and twisting off meat.

Giganotosaurus, the biggest meat eater of all, preys on a giant plant eater, Rebbachisaurus. *Dinosaurs almost identical to these South American ones lived in North Africa at the same time.*

HOLOCENE EPOCH

TRIASSIC PERIOD · JURASSIC PERIOD · CRETACEOUS PERIOD · PALEOCENE AND EOCENE EPOCHS · OLIGOCENE, MIOCENE, AND PLIOCENE EPOCHS · PLEISTOCENE EPOCH

NEW SLICERS AND SLASHERS

A deadly new breed of hunter, the "raptor" dinosaur, emerged during the Cretaceous period. These dinosaurs ranged in size from a poodle to a truck, but all had sharp teeth and a curved "killer" claw on each hand and foot. Giant raptor dinosaurs have recently been discovered from Utah to Japan, and a raptorlike giant, *Megaraptor*, was recently found in Argentina. While not a true raptor, *Megaraptor* sported a 2-foot- (60-cm-) long claw on each limb.

SUPER CHEWERS

The best chewers the world has ever known were the duck-billed dinosaurs. They evolved from iguanodont dinosaurs and sported as many as 800 teeth set in comblike rows. When one set of teeth ground down on tough plants, another set was always ready to replace them. And duckbill jaws chewed in three directions—up and down, in and out, *and* sideways—like an accordion.

Utahraptor, the largest "raptor" dinosaur, readies its attack on an armored Gastonia *110 million years ago.*

PLANT EATERS

While sauropod dinosaurs continued to thunder across much of the planet, new kinds of bird-hipped dinosaurs evolved. Armored dinosaurs grew as big as tanks. So did horned dinosaurs, such as *Triceratops* and *Achelousaurus* in North America.

A speedy ornithomimid meat eater dashes by Achelousaurus, *a horned plant eater that lived 70 million years ago in the American West.*

THE RISE OF MAMMALS

Mammals were alive through dinosaur times. For millions of years, they were primitive and small. Some may have laid eggs. In the Cretaceous period, mammals began to change.

Nearly 70 million years ago mammals broke off into two major groups. One group was placental mammals, which give birth to well-developed babies. The other mammal group was marsupials, which give birth to tiny babies that crawl into the mother's pouch to nurse. Both groups are alive today, but the first kinds of each group are long extinct.

Among the placental mammals of late dinosaur times were the first primates. Monkeys, apes, and humans are some of today's primates. But the first primates, such as *Purgatorius*, were mouse-sized creatures. Scientists can tell that they are primates by their molar teeth, which look much like the back teeth of modern primates.

An Albertosaurus dinosaur growls in the background while a mouse-sized Alphadon mammal watches carefully from a tree branch in western Canada 75 million years ago.

HOW DO YOU KNOW IT WAS A MAMMAL?

Mammals are different from other animals in many ways. They have hair and are warm-blooded. Their hearts have four chambers, and most don't lay eggs. All mammals nurse their babies.

But you can't see those features in a fossil. So scientists look to bones. Mammal skulls have a special jaw joint and a variety of different kinds of teeth, including grinding molars. Primitive mammals have a jaw joint that didn't exist in their cynodont ancestors.

The cynodont jaw and teeth are simple in construction.

The mammal jaw has a more complex joint.

WHY MORE MAMMALS?

It was long thought that mammals didn't have the chance to develop into many forms until after dinosaurs disappeared from the scene at the end of the Cretaceous period. But new evidence suggests that mammals began to evolve into many new kinds several million years before dinosaurs died out. What caused the rise of mammals? Scientists now think that the movement of continents and the lowering of sea levels provided new territory where new kinds of mammals could emerge.

Purgatorius *was one of the first primates. It was about 4 inches (10 cm) long and probably ate insects.*

THE DINOSAURS DISAPPEAR: THE CRETACEOUS EXTINCTION

The dinosaurs disappeared from the land 65 million years ago. So did many other kinds of animals in the oceans and skies, including giant sea reptiles and flying reptiles. Scientists have offered many theories for the death of the dinosaurs—from freezing weather to gassy stomachs. In the last ten years increasing evidence suggests one answer, at least as the last and worst change of an ever harsher environment. A huge asteroid crashed into the Gulf of Mexico. The impact sent enormous tidal waves across the earth and started many fires. Clouds of dust and ash blackened the sky, blocking sunlight and cooling the planet. Volcanic explosions may have produced the same effects. Many animals couldn't cope with the weather changes. But mysteriously, birds and mammals, crocodiles, and many other animals survived.

ALBERTOSAURUS
al-**buhrt**-oh-**sor**-uhs
NAME: "Alberta reptile," for Alberta, Canada, where it was first found
TIME: 80 million to 75 million years ago
FOSSILS FOUND: western North America
SIZE: 25 feet (7.5 m) long
An early member of the tyrannosaur family. Tyrannosaurs were among the last and most fearsome dinosaur meat eaters. They had only 2 fingers on small hands, but huge heads and powerful jaws.

AMARGASAURUS
uh-**mahr**-gah-**sor**-uhs
NAME: "Amarga reptile," for La Amarga Creek, Argentina
TIME: 115 million years ago
FOSSILS FOUND: South America
SIZE: 30 feet (9 m) long
This odd plant-eating dinosaur had a double mane of long spines down its back. What it used this bony sail for is not known.

ARCHELON ▶

ahr-kuh-lahn
NAME: "ruler turtle," for its gigantic size
TIME: 65 million years ago
FOSSILS FOUND: western North America
SIZE: 12 feet (3.6 m) long
This giant turtle had a light shell probably covered with thick skin. Its paddle legs helped it "fly" through water as a penguin does. It probably ate jellyfish.

AVIMIMUS ▶
ah-vee-**mim**-uhs
NAME: "bird mimic," because it looks so much like a bird
TIME: 85 million to 75 million years ago
FOSSILS FOUND: Mongolia
SIZE: 5 feet (1.5 m) long
A toothless descendent of sharp-toothed, meat-eating dinosaurs. It was among the fastest of the dinosaurs and may have lived on insects. We don't know whether it was feathered, as some dinosaurs were.

▼ BARYONYX
bayr-ee-**awn**-iks
NAME: "heavy claw"
TIME: 125 million years ago
FOSSILS FOUND: England
SIZE: 30 feet (9 m) long
It had strange crocodile-like teeth and claws 1 foot (30 cm) long. It may have lived by snaring fish with its claws and jaws.

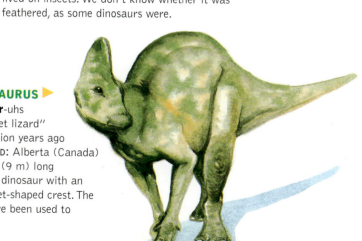

CORYTHOSAURUS ▶
kor-**ith**-uh-**sor**-uhs
NAME: "helmet lizard"
TIME: 70 million years ago
FOSSILS FOUND: Alberta (Canada)
SIZE: 30 feet (9 m) long
A duck-billed dinosaur with an unusual helmet-shaped crest. The crest may have been used to make sounds.

DEINOSUCHUS ▶

die-noh-**sook**-uhs
NAME: "terrible crocodile"
TIME: 65 million years ago
FOSSILS FOUND: western North America
SIZE: 50 feet (15 m) long
One of the biggest meat eaters ever, longer than the biggest carnivorous dinosaur of its world, *T. rex*. Perhaps it ate dinosaurs.

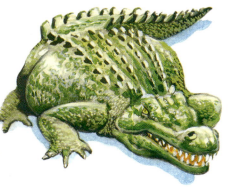

ICHTHYORNIS ▶

ik-thee-**or**-nis
NAME: "fish bird," because the bones in its spine were cup-shaped at both ends as in fish, not saddle-shaped as in modern birds
TIME: 87 million to 74 million years ago
FOSSILS FOUND: Kansas and Texas (USA)
SIZE: 8 inches (20 cm) tall
When it was found in the 1870s, this shore bird's toothed jaws were mistaken for the similar jaws of a fish-eating sea reptile. It was a strong flier with a big head and bill.

▼ MOSASAURUS

moh-suh-**sor**-uhs
NAME: "Meuse River lizard," because the first skull was found near the Meuse River in Holland
TIME: 80 million to 65 million years ago
FOSSILS FOUND: Europe, North America
SIZE: up to 40 feet (12 m) long.
The first giant reptile from dinosaur times ever found (1780), it was related to modern lizards such as the Komodo dragon.

EUOPLOCEPHALUS ▶

yoo-oh-ploh-**sef**-uh-luhs
NAME: "well-armored head"
TIME: 75 million years ago
FOSSILS FOUND: western North America
SIZE: 18 feet (5.4 m) long
The best known of all armored dinosaurs, this ankylosaur was covered with armor— even on its eyelids! It was toothless but used its beak to cut plants.

IGUANODON ▶

i-**gwahn**-uh-dahn
NAME: "iguana tooth"
TIME: 135 million to 110 million years ago
FOSSILS FOUND: Europe, North America, Asia, North Africa
SIZE: 33 feet (10 m) long
Best known for its distinctive thumb spike. Iguanodon was one of the first dinosaurs found in the 1820s. Originally scientists thought the spike stuck out from its head.

◀ TRICERATOPS

trie-**sair**-uh-tahps
NAME: "three-horned face"
TIME: 65 million years ago
FOSSILS FOUND: western North America
SIZE: 25 feet (7.5 m) long
The largest horned dinosaur and perhaps the most common. It may have weighed as much as 5 tons.

CHAPTER 9

MAMMALS AGAINST BIRDS
Paleocene and Eocene Epochs—65 million to 35 million years ago

After the dinosaurs died, giant flightless birds battled meat-eating mammals for domination of the land. During the Paleocene epoch, the birds were in charge. Some were enormous—far larger than the meat-eating mammals of the time. The first hoofed mammals also appeared during this period. Some were meat eaters, like the wolf-sized *Mesonyx*. Others were plant eaters. Since there were no grasslands yet, these animals were not grazers like today's hoofed animals. Instead they browsed on trees or dug for roots.

Nine-foot- (3-m-) high Diatryma digs its powerful beak into the cat-sized creodont Tritemnodon. Diatryma was the king predator of its world. But these birds were soon replaced by faster, smarter predators—mammals.

40 million years equals one inch.

► Giant meat-eating birds stalk the land
► First hoofed plant eaters develop
► First whales enter the sea

CLAM UP AND GO FISH

In the oceans of 60 million years ago, the huge-shelled ammonites that had been so common in dinosaur times had disappeared. In their place were many clamlike mollusks and sea urchins. Five-foot- (1.5-m-) long ratfish and other sharks were common, too. A new wave of fish evolution just before and after the end of dinosaurs produced modern bony fishes. Trout and salmon are survivors from this time. *Enchodus* was not. It was a 7-inch (17.5-cm) salmonlike fish with huge teeth that closed like a trap. *Hypsidoris* was a freshwater ancestor of goldfish and minnows. It grew to be 8 inches (20 cm) long. And judging by the tiny bones in its ears, *Hypsidoris* had a good sense of hearing. *Eobothus* was one of the first flat fish like today's flounder. It fed along the ocean floor and grew to be 4 inches (10 cm) long.

GOOD-BYE TO SOUTH AMERICA

South America and Antarctica were separated from the rest of the world by water at this time. In isolation, the southern lands developed many strange animals. Among the first were armadillos and their relatives, which later grew to be as big as hippopotamuses.

A sharp-toothed Enchodus *and larger* Hypsidoris *swim along the sea floor.*

TRIASSIC PERIOD   JURASSIC PERIOD   CRETACEOUS PERIOD   PALEOCENE AND EOCENE EPOCHS   OLIGOCENE, MIOCENE, AND PLIOCENE EPOCHS   PLEISTOCENE EPOCH

HOLOCENE EPOCH

x20

MAMMALS TAKE THE LAND

Mammals finally became the ruling land animals 50 million years ago, during the Eocene epoch. The first hunting mammals were heavily built creodonts with clawed feet, long tails, and small brains.

Also alive at this time was the biggest meat-eating mammal ever. Its name was *Andrewsarchus* and it was among the last of the condylarths—mammals that had small brains. As grasses began to spread across the land, condylarths were replaced by grazers. These grazers included horses, rhinoceroses, pigs, aardvarks, and several other mammal groups, now extinct.

A pack of powerful, meat-eating Andrewsarchus *run in search of prey. While their exact appearance remains a mystery, these early mammalian hunters are known to have had large heads and powerful jaws.*

MAMMALS FLY!

Bats, the only flying mammals, first appeared more than 35 million years ago. The skeleton of the oldest extinct bat, *Icaronycteris*, was found by accident in rocks from an ancient Wyoming lake. It already showed many features of modern bats, including a diet of insects. Like many of today's bats, these ancient fliers probably located their food by producing echoing sound waves.

SMART AND DUMB

Modern mammals, including people, are the smartest animals ever—with the biggest brains for their bodies. Most dinosaurs (especially the big ones) were pretty pea-brained. But some dinosaurs had bigger brains, such as the man-sized meat eater *Troodon*. Mammals took a while to catch up to *Troodon* in braininess. Even after dinosaurs died out, many of the new and bigger mammals, like *Uintatherium*, were no brainier than the big dinosaurs.

Pachyaena

Ambulocetus

Rodhocetus

BACK TO THE SEA!

Here come the mammals!—and not just on land and in the air. For the first time, about 50 million years ago, there were mammals in the ocean—the first whales.

Recent fossil discoveries show us how some land animals evolved into ocean-dwelling whales in the Eocene epoch. In the space of just 20 million years, 8-foot- (2.4-m-) long walking mammals that ate fish at the water's edge developed into whales the size and shape of those today.

Streamside mammals, called mesonychids, included *Pachyaena*. Mesonychids were probably the group from which the land ancestors of whales evolved. One of these ancestors was *Ambulocetus*, a creature that lived half on land and half in the sea 50 million years ago. *Ambulocetus* fossils were found in Pakistan. They still had hooves on

Basilosaurus

Orca

their four feet for walking, but their feet were so big they could work as swimming paddles.

Three million years after *Ambulocetus* came *Rodhocetus,* also 8 feet (2.4 m) long but with a more streamlined body and a big, flexible tail for swimming like a whale, though it could still walk on land.

Ten million years later, the deep seas were home to a 50-foot (15-m) whale, *Basilosaurus,* whose limbs were tiny and useless. Dolphins had also appeared by this time. As today's dolphins do, early dolphins used sounds to find their way through the sea.

A WHALE OF A TOOTH

The earliest whale, *Pakecetus,* had saw-edged teeth for slicing meat. That was a clue to scientists that its ancestors were bearlike meat eaters that lived on land soon after dinosaurs died out.

▼ CHRIACUS
crie-ak-uhs
NAME: "puncture point," because its teeth had sharp, pointed cusps
TIME: 63 million to 53 million years ago
FOSSILS FOUND: western North America
SIZE: 3 feet (1 m) long
The most primitive ungulates included this agile tree climber, which could grip with its tail. It ate insects, fruit, and small animals. It walked like a bear, with its entire foot striking the ground.

▼ ENCHODUS
enk-oh-duhs
NAME: "spear tooth"
TIME: 70 million to 57 million years ago
FOSSILS FOUND: worldwide
SIZE: 7 inches (17.5 cm) long
One of the advanced bony fish that include today's trout and salmon. It had a big head and eyes and was a fast-swimming hunter of other ocean fish.

◀ MIACIS
mie-ak-is *or* **mie**-a-sis
NAME: "lesser point," because its teeth were smaller than some creodonts' teeth
TIME: 63 million to 50 million years ago
FOSSILS FOUND: Europe
SIZE: 8 inches (20 cm) long
This weasel-like animal was built for climbing trees and hunting small animals. It was related to dogs, lions, and bears, not to creodonts.

▼ PALEOTRIONYX
pay-lee-oh-**trie**-oh-niks
NAME: "ancient three claw"
TIME: 65 million to 57 million years ago
FOSSILS FOUND: western North America
SIZE: 18 inches (45 cm) long
This freshwater turtle featured a shell covered with skin, not hard plates, and a long mobile neck. It probably ate everything it could, from weeds to fish.

◀ PLANETETHERIUM

pla-**neet**-uh-**theer**-ee-uhm
NAME: "wanderer beast"
TIME: 60 million years ago
FOSSILS FOUND: western North America
SIZE: 10 inches (25 cm) long
A squirrel-sized mammal. Its skin may have been webbed between its legs and tail, helping it to glide between trees.

▼ DIACODEXIS
die-**ak**-oh-**dek**-sis
NAME: "two point biter," for the 2 cusps
on its premolar teeth
TIME: 50 million years ago
FOSSILS FOUND: Europe, Asia, North America
SIZE: 20 inches (50 cm) long
This earliest known ancestor of modern pigs had
5 toes and lived in the forest. It had long legs
built for running and may have been the fastest-
running animal of its time.

EOBASILEUS ▶
ee-oh-ba-**sil**-ee-uhs
NAME: "dawn (Eocene) king," because it was one
of the largest animals during the Eocene epoch
TIME: 37 million years ago
FOSSILS FOUND: North America
SIZE: 10 feet (3 m) long
One of the uintatheres, the largest plant eaters of
the time. Its head had bony knobs as well as horns
made of hair, like rhinoceros horns.

▲ METACHEIROMYS
met-uh-**kie**-roh-mis
NAME: "next to the aye-aye," because the
scientist who first saw the bones mistakenly
thought the animal was a primate with hands like
the aye-aye, a lemur that lives in Madagascar
TIME: 45 million years ago
FOSSILS FOUND: North America
SIZE: 18 inches (45 cm) long
This short-legged animal had sharp claws, a
heavy tail, and a head something like an
armadillo's. It lived in forests and dug for roots
with its large front claws.

NEOCATHARTES ▶
nee-oh-kuh-**thahr**-teez
NAME: "new vulture," because it
seemed to be an early relative of
the New World turkey vulture
TIME: 37 million to 33 million
years ago
FOSSILS FOUND: western
North America
SIZE: 18 inches (45 cm) long
A lightly built bird that could fly but spent most of
its time on the ground, hunting rodents and small
reptiles with its sharp beak and claws.

◀ SARKASTODON
sahr-**kas**-toh-dahn
NAME: "flesh-tearing tooth"
TIME: 37 million years ago
FOSSILS FOUND: Mongolia
SIZE: 10 feet (3 m) long
This bear-sized animal was the
largest of the creodonts, the
dominant meat eaters of this time.

CHAPTER 10

MAMMALS RULE

Oligocene, Miocene, and Pliocene Epochs—35 million to 1.6 million years ago

Many large mammals appeared 35 million years ago, as world temperatures cooled and grasslands replaced forests. But the biggest animals were not the fiercest. The fastest, smartest, and nastiest land creatures of the time were small hunters that ate even smaller prey. The killers were the first saber-tooths, less than 5 feet (1.5 m) long. Among their victims may have been weasels, hamsters, and beavers, all of which appeared at this time.

A vicious 4-foot-(1.2-m-) long hunter, Nimravus, *battles a saber-toothed* Eusmilus. *This scene is based on an actual fossil* Nimravus *skull, which appears to have been punctured by* Eusmilus *teeth.*

40 million years equals one inch.

WHO WAS THE BIGGEST?

Biggest of all animals of this time was a hornless rhinoceros named *Indricotherium*. It was the biggest land mammal ever. Looking like a cross between a giraffe and a rhino, it was 16 feet (4.8 m) tall and weighed 15 tons! The titanotheres were also enormous. They had begun as small piglike mammals, but by now were huge plant eaters, like the "thunder beast" *Brontotherium*.

Who ate these animals? Pack-hunting ancestors of dogs, perhaps.

Brontotherium like these two may have locked horns in a test of strength to win mates or territory.

MEANWHILE, IN SOUTH AMERICA . . .

Still cut off from the rest of the world, South America developed its own strange animals. Some of these marsupial mammals looked, by chance, much like wolves and bears. One such animal was the 5-foot- (1.5-m-) long bearlike *Borhyaena*. Heavily built horselike and camel-like animals were its prey. It may also have eaten the large armadillos of the time, if it could penetrate the giant armadillo's armor.

HOLOCENE EPOCH

TRIASSIC PERIOD | JURASSIC PERIOD | CRETACEOUS PERIOD | PALEOCENE AND EOCENE EPOCHS | OLIGOCENE, MIOCENE, AND PLIOCENE EPOCHS | PLEISTOCENE EPOCH

x20

PIGS ON STILTS, GIANT CAMELS, AND PLENTY OF HORSES

The earth was changing fast during the Miocene epoch, 20 million years ago, and so were the animals on it. Soon after, in the Eocene epoch, India collided with Asia, pushing up the Himalayan Mountains and Tibetan Plateau. Now other mountains were rising, too: the Andes in South America and the Rockies in the American West. But these building mountains were not barriers to the movement of new groups of animals.

Horses, camels up to 10 feet (3 m) high, rhinoceroses, and many now-extinct groups of animals were developing in North America, including saber-toothed cats and oreodonts. Oreodonts resembled pigs but had long legs and so grew more than 4 feet (1.2 m) high. Chalicotheres looked like horses with big claws. They grew to 10 feet long (3 m) but could not run as fast as horses. Doglike mammals entered the sea and became ancestors of seals, sea lions, and walruses.

In Africa, the last of the creodont hunters included the giant, wolflike *Megistotherium*. Weighing one ton, it may have been the biggest meat-eating mammal ever.

Moropus browses on tree leaves at the edge of a river where a hippopotamus-like *Teleoceras* feeds. *Osteoborus, a heavyset scavenging dog less than 3 feet (90 cm) long, feeds on a carcass of a dead* Synthetoceras, *a deerlike early camel.*

Mother and child Hyracotherium, *the earliest of horses*

HORSING AROUND

The first horselike animal appeared nearly 50 million years ago. Sometimes called Eohippus, "the dawn horse," this animal is truly named *Hyracotherium*. It was just 2 feet (60 cm) long and lived on many continents until 35 million years ago, when its line died out everywhere but in North America. There, Eohippus evolved into the more lightly built 4-foot- (1.2-m-) long *Mesohippus*.

When the climate dried and grasslands spread 20 million years ago, the now-extinct ancestors of modern horses, zebras, and asses evolved in North America and again spread across the world. Like other groups of animals, horses produced many different forms. Some kinds of horses went extinct completely. Others led, over time, to the living animal we know as the modern horse.

HORSING AROUND AND NOT AROUND

Though much of the development of horses took place in North America, horses disappeared from the continent 11,000 years ago. Their end was mysterious, perhaps caused by an epidemic of disease. Only 400 years ago, horses returned to North America, brought by humans from Europe.

HORSES THROUGH TIME

The development of horses followed many lines to the present. Here are some well-known ancestors of today's horses.

Mesohippus *was slim in build and only 4 feet (1.2 m) long. Its weight was carried across its spread toes.*

Parahippus *was more than 3 feet (1 m) high at the shoulder. It was larger than* Mesohippus, *with a similar body. But its molar teeth were shaped like grinding stones, better designed for chewing grasses than those of its ancestors.*

Merychippus *followed. It was similar to* Parahippus *in size, but it had more teeth designed for grinding and ate only grass. Like earlier horses it had three toes, but now only the middle toe carried weight.*

Hipparion *was less than 5 feet (1.5 m) long. It looked like a modern horse, though it had three toes.*

THE BRIDGE OPENS

The Pliocene epoch, around five million to less than two million years ago, was the time when continents, plants, and many animals took on their modern form. South America and North America joined once more. Many animals that are still alive today made the move from continent to continent. Armadillos, porcupines, and opossums came north. Horses, pumas, dogs, and rabbits went south. But the bridge between continents was also crossed successfully by many now-extinct animals. Mastodons went south, and armored glyptodonts and giant ground sloths came north.

A saber-toothed Homotherium *stalks a baby mammoth. This scene may have happened just as it appears. In a Texas cave, scientists discovered the bones of young and adult saber-toothed cats among the fossils of young mammoths. The cats had unusually sharp and short canine teeth, perfect for killing mammoths, extinct relatives of elephants. Designed for strength and power, these cats could not run fast. But mammoths could not run quickly, either. When mammoths died out several thousand years ago, so did* Homotherium.

FROM DOGS TO SEA LIONS

Forty million years ago, a group of meat eaters called arctoids broke off into four very different families. All had the same shape of middle ear, uncovered claws, and less specialized teeth than those of cats. But, beyond that, each group became very different. One included dogs and wolves, another weasels, otters, and badgers. A third included bears and the giant panda. And the last were raccoons and several other mammals.

Then, 25 million years ago, the strangest change of all took place. Some arctoids became sleek, with webbed limbs and teeth made for catching fish and clams. These were the pinnipeds, seals and walruses. One of the earliest was *Allodesmus*, a sea lion relative that resembled the biggest earless seal today—the sea elephant.

Allodesmus was among the first known members of the sea lion family. But already it had the key features we recognize in pinnipeds— webbed limbs, flexible necks, and teeth designed for catching fish.

◀ AMPHICYON

am-fi-**sie**-awn
NAME: "near dog," because its teeth were like a dog's teeth, though its body resembled a bear's
TIME: 30 million to 23 million years ago
FOSSILS FOUND: Europe, North America
SIZE: 6½ feet (2 m) long
This "bear-dog" was one of a successful group of big hunters. It may have eaten both plants and animals, just as bears do today.

▲ ARGENTAVIS

ahr-gen-**tay**-vis
NAME: "Argentina bird"
TIME: 3 million years ago
FOSSILS FOUND: South America
SIZE: 5 feet (1.5 m) high, 24-foot (7.2-m) wingspan
A vulture bigger than any other flying bird ever! It was twice the size of the albatross—the longest-winged bird alive today.

◀ ARSINOITHERIUM

ahr-**sin**-oh-i-**theer**-ee-uhm
NAME: "Arsinoe's beast," for the famous Egyptian queen Arsinoe, who gave her name to the region where the fossil was found
TIME: 8 million years ago
FOSSILS FOUND: North Africa
SIZE: 11½ feet (3.5 m) long
This enormous browser only looked like a rhinoceros. Its "horn" was hollow, and its teeth were designed to chew tough riverside plants.

▼ DRYOPITHECUS

drie-oh-**pi**-thi-kuhs
NAME: "tree ape"
TIME: 20 million to 5 million years ago
FOSSILS FOUND: Europe, Asia, Africa
SIZE: 2 feet (60 cm) long
Built like a chimpanzee, it could walk on 4 legs or just 2. It climbed trees and ate fruit.

▼ GERANOPTERUS

jair-uhn-**ahp**-tuhr-us
NAME: "crane wing"
TIME: 35 million to 30 million years ago
FOSSILS FOUND: Europe
SIZE: up to 6 inches (15 cm) long
These colorful birds nested in holes. They were the most common birds on and over the land in the Oligocene epoch, the middle epoch of the Tertiary period.

INDRICOTHERIUM

in-drik-oh-**theer**-ee-uhm
NAME: "indrik beast," for the mythical animal in old Russian stories and poems
TIME: 30 million years ago
FOSSILS FOUND: Asia
SIZE: 26 feet (7.8 m) long
The largest land mammal ever. It weighed 15 tons, more than the biggest elephant. It probably browsed like a giraffe on treetop foliage.

PHORUSRHACUS ▶

for-uhs-**rak**-uhs
NAME: "wrinkle-bearer," first named for a lower jaw with a rough surface, supposedly belonging to a ground sloth, which was later found to be the jaw of a giant flightless bird
TIME: 27 million years ago
FOSSILS FOUND: South America
SIZE: 5 (1.5 m) feet high
Flightless birds were the chief hunters in South America after the dinosaurs died out. This powerful runner with a huge head and beak was well built for ripping flesh.

◀ PYROTHERIUM

pie-roh-**theer**-ee-uhm
NAME: "fire beast"
TIME: 35 million years ago
FOSSILS FOUND: South America
SIZE: 10 feet (3 m) long
Though these animals looked like elephants, they are not related.

SYNDYOCERAS ▶

sin-die-oh-**seer**-uhs *or* **sin**-die-**os**-er-uhs
NAME: "two together horn," for the forked horn on its nose
TIME: 23 million to 5 million years ago
FOSSILS FOUND: North America
SIZE: 4 feet (1.2 m) long
One of the group called protoceratids, it was a primitive plant-chewing mammal with strange horns. Only its third and fourth toes could move.

◀ TELICOMYS

tel-**ik**-oh-mis
NAME: "ultimate mouse," because it was a huge rodent
TIME: 25 million to 5 million years ago
FOSSILS FOUND: South America
SIZE: 7 feet (2.1 m) long
The biggest rodent that ever lived was the size of an ox. It had a thick tail.

CHAPTER 11

COLD TIMES, HARD TIMES

Pleistocene Epoch—1.6 million to 10,000 years ago

What we call the Ice Age was not one event, but a string of ice ages broken up by warmer periods. During warm periods, the world's climate was warmer than it is today. During the cold periods, sheets of ice covered huge areas of North America, northern Europe, and western South America.

Around the world lived mammoths and mastodons. Woolly rhinoceroses grazed in Europe. Twenty-foot- (6-m-) long giant ground sloths reached high into trees to feed in South America. Giant beavers and wolves ranged across North America.

The La Brea tar pits in what is now Los Angeles were pools of liquid tar 14,000 to 4,000 years ago. Thousands of animals, including mammoths, camels, lions, and the short-faced bear, were trapped and died there.

40 million years equals one inch.

◀ PRECAMBRIAN ERA | CAMBRIAN PERIOD | ORDOVICIAN PERIOD | SILURIAN AND DEVONIAN PERIODS | CARBONIFEROUS AND PERMIAN PERIODS

ELEPHANT RELATIVES

Some animals adapted to the cold lived on in Asia and Europe all through the Ice Ages. These included mammoths and mastodons, among the largest mammals ever to live on land. Mastodons lived in North American forests eight million years ago. Mammoths first appeared in Africa five million years ago, then spread to northern continents. The last of them died out just 3,700 years ago. The long hair and thick underfur of woolly mammoths kept them warm even in the freezing Arctic. Their tusks curved up and back, and they grew to a height of nearly 10 feet (3 m). The biggest fossil mammoth ever found was 14 feet (4.2 m) high at the shoulder.

Mammoth

Mastodon

MAMMOTH SOUP

Mammoths have been found so well preserved in the ice of Siberia that if their remains were thawed out, you could make soup from their bones and gnaw on their meat. The thick hair is still preserved on many of these mummies.

GIANTS DOWN UNDER

In Pleistocene times, Australia was home to animals as remarkable as today's kangaroos, koalas, and wombats. But some were far larger! An ancestor of modern kangaroos, *Procoptodon*, grew to 10 feet (3 m) long. Other plant eaters included the 8-foot- (2.4-m-) long *Palorchestes*, which may have had a long trunk. *Diprotodon* was the largest plant-eating marsupial of all, the size of a rhinoceros. It ate bushes it scraped from the ground with its big paws. The plant eaters were prey for *Thylacoleo*, a lionlike marsupial hunter.

Procoptodon, a huge primitive kangaroo, is attacked by Thylacoleo, *a lionlike marsupial.*

THE RISE OF HUMANS

A fierce new predator had arrived on the scene by the start of the Pleistocene epoch—the human being. Prehistoric humans were neither big nor fast, but they used a dangerous combination of brainpower and carefully crafted weapons against the giant plant eaters of the time.

The earliest known ancestors of humans appeared during the Pliocene epoch, over four million years ago. The best-known and most complete fossil of an early humanlike primate is the 3.5-million-year-old "Lucy." Lucy is a skeleton of a grown female the size of a modern six-year-old girl. She belongs to a species of *Australopithecus*, the group of primates that anthropologists think led to modern humans.

Tiny Australopithecus afarensis *walked upright 3.5 million years ago.*

Homo habilis *was making stone tools less than 2 million years ago.*

Homo erectus *conquered fire at least 1.5 million years ago.*

After Lucy's time, *Australopithecus* took on different forms. One species was sturdy and over 5½ feet (1.7 m) tall. Another was built like today's humans, but stood only as tall as a chimpanzee.

True humans first appeared less than two million years ago. *Homo habilis*, "handy human" (also found in Africa), was less than 5 feet (1.5 m) tall, with a heavy jaw and ridges on its brow. It made tools, including cutting blades from flakes of stone.

Several other kinds of early humans appeared about 1.5 million years ago. *Homo erectus* ("upright human"), a wandering hunter, tool maker, and fire user, spread from Africa through Europe and Asia.

Around 200,000 years ago, Neanderthals appeared. They were short, powerful humans with big heads and brains bigger than ours. Neanderthals lived alongside modern humans (*Homo sapiens*) for almost 70,000 years, then died out mysteriously around 30,000 years ago.

Homo sapiens like us first appeared in Africa around 100,000 years ago or even earlier. For a long time they made stone tools the same way Neanderthals did. Then 35,000 years ago, human culture began to change. In Europe one group of modern humans, called Cro-Magnons, started making new kinds of clothes, tools, and weapons. They became much better hunters. Like no humans before, they painted animals on the insides of caves and carved animal decorations in bone. Modern humans in other places began doing similar kinds of things. By the end of the Pleistocene, people had developed languages, had spread around the world, and had even taken up farming.

LOSE A DOG, FIND A TREASURE

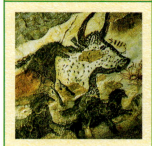

Four boys were looking for their dog in southern France in 1940. While searching, they stumbled across the greatest series of cave paintings ever found. Lascaux is the site of spectacularly colorful paintings of animals hunted by Cro-Magnon people.

Neanderthals had an advanced culture: They played flutes, carved wood, and gathered flowers.

Cro-Magnons made colorful cave paintings just 30,000 years ago.

WEAPONS OR GERMS? THE PLEISTOCENE EXTINCTION

About 12,000 years ago, many giant animals of the New World were wiped out in the space of just a few hundred years. Scientists have suggested that this was the first man-made extinction. Early human hunters from Asia came to North and South America at this time and may have killed off animals unprepared for such clever predators.

But the latest theories suggest that something else that humans brought to the Americas killed these animals—diseases. The spread of new germs, helped along by human hunters, may have wiped out the giant Ice Age mammals of the Americas.

▶ CASTOROIDES
cas-tor-**oi**-deez
NAME: "beaverlike"
TIME: 3 million to 9,000 years ago
FOSSILS FOUND: North America
SIZE: 7 feet (2 m) long
This giant beaver lived on land and was the size of a black bear.

▼ FELIS LEO SPELAEA
feel-is **lee**-oh spel-**ay**-uh
NAME: "cave lion cat"
TIME: 600,000 to 10,000 years ago
FOSSILS FOUND: Europe
SIZE: 10 feet (3 m) long
This giant cave lion was ⅓ larger than the biggest lion today. It killed with its sharp teeth and powerful bite.

▲ ELASMOTHERIUM
e-**las**-moh-**theer**-ee-uhm
NAME: "plated beast," for the enamel plates on its teeth
TIME: 1.6 million to 12,000 years ago
FOSSILS FOUND: eastern Europe, western Asia
SIZE: 16 feet (4.8 m) long
The size of an elephant, this Ice Age rhinoceros had a horn 6½ feet (2 m) long. It was hairy like the smaller woolly rhinoceros, which shared its cold habitat.

◀ MACRAUCHENIA
mak-raw-**keen**-ee-uh
NAME: "long neck"
TIME: 2 million to 11,000 years ago
FOSSILS FOUND: South America
SIZE: 8 feet (2.4 m) high
One of many strange hoofed animals that evolved in isolated South America. This camel-sized animal may have had a trunk.

▼ GLYPTODON
glip-toh-dahn
NAME: "carved tooth," for the deep grooves in its teeth
TIME: 1.6 million to 11,000 years ago
FOSSILS FOUND: South America
SIZE: 10 feet (3 m) long
A giant relative of the plant-eating armadillos. Armor covered its head, body, and even its thick tail.

MASTODON ▶

mas-tuh-dahn
NAME: "breast tooth," for the large, rounded cusps on its teeth
TIME: 7 million to 8,000 years ago
FOSSILS FOUND: North America
SIZE: 10 feet (3 m) high
This relative of the elephant lived in American forests until 12,000 years ago. Its tusks were long and curved.

◀ MEGALOCEROS

may-guh-loh-**seer**-uhs
NAME: "giant horn"
TIME: 500,000 to 11,000 years ago
FOSSILS FOUND: eastern Europe and western Asia
SIZE: 7 feet (2 m) high with horns 10 feet (3 m) across
Called the "Irish Elk," this was a giant deer that died out 11,000 years ago in Ireland.

MEGATHERIUM ▶

meg-uh-**theer**-ee-uhm
NAME: "great animal"
TIME: 2 million to 11,000 years ago
FOSSILS FOUND: South America to southeastern North America
SIZE: 20 feet (6 m) long
A ground sloth the size of an elephant that fed on treetops by propping itself up on its powerful tail.

▼ PLATYGONUS

plat-ee-**goh**-nuhs
NAME: "broad angle," for the shape of its lower jaw
TIME: 3 million to 10,000 years ago
FOSSILS FOUND: North and South America
SIZE: 3 feet 3 inches (1 m) long
Related to modern piglike peccaries, its skull was unusually short and deep with 2 big teeth for digging up plants.

◀ TOXODON

toks-oh-dahn
NAME: "bow tooth," for the arched shape of its molar teeth
TIME: 3 million to 11,000 years ago
FOSSILS FOUND: South America
SIZE: 9 feet (2.7 m) long
Like a black rhinoceros, this plant eater may have had a fleshy, grasping lip for eating plants.

People lived in a world rich in plant and animal life for most of the last ten thousand years, at least in places where modern human hunters had not yet settled. Even as recently as two hundred years ago, huge flocks of passenger pigeons swarmed over North America. Enormous herds of buffalo roamed the plains. Giant flightless birds inhabited islands in the Southern Hemisphere. The sight of gun-carrying humans was not a source of fear to these creatures. It should have been.

The dodo was a 50-pound (23-kg) flightless bird that lived on the island of Réunion in the Indian Ocean. In the 1500s, sailors came to Réunion. In 150 years, all the dodos were gone—killed to provide oil for people and food for their pigs and dogs.

40 million years equals one inch.

EASY SHOT

The handsome passenger pigeon flew across the forests of the American Midwest in unbelievable numbers just a century ago. Flocks of pigeons were so huge that the skies would turn dark for days on end as they flew over by the billions.

But the passenger pigeon had the misfortune of making an easy target and tasty meal for shotgun-wielding hunters. A single shot would bring down several birds at a time from their huge flocks. A hunting expedition would easily take in pigeons by the barrel.

By early in the twentieth century, the once-common passenger pigeon was rare. By the 1930s, just a single pigeon, nicknamed Martha, lived on in a Cincinnati zoo. When Martha died, the passenger pigeon was gone forever.

THE YOLK'S ON ALL OF US

Until recently, islands were home to enormous flightless birds that laid equally enormous eggs. The largest egg ever laid was produced by *Aepyornis*, a 10-foot- (3-m-) tall bird from Madagascar. This flightless bird, also known as the elephant bird, weighed over 1,000 pounds (450 kg) and laid eggs 1 foot (30 cm) long, weighing 20 pounds (9 kg) and holding 20 pints (9.4 liters) of yolk.

A century ago, flocks of passenger pigeons made for easy hunting. Even the worst marksman could collect a barrelful in minutes.

HOLOCENE EPOCH

TRIASSIC PERIOD   JURASSIC PERIOD   CRETACEOUS PERIOD   PALEOCENE AND EOCENE EPOCHS   OLIGOCENE, MIOCENE, AND PLIOCENE EPOCHS   PLEISTOCENE EPOCH

GOING, GOING, GONE

In the last ten thousand years, humans have wiped out animals faster than creatures have disappeared at any time in Earth's history.

There are many causes of human-made extinction. Hunting and fishing for food, clothing, and fun are only some of the most direct ways we've wiped out entire species. By introducing new and unfamiliar predators, we upset delicate environments, especially on islands where life has evolved for a long time in isolation.

But the greatest damage to life-forms happens when we ruin the habitats in which animals live. Spreading cities, pollution, farming, ranching, and cutting down trees for wood all destroy the wilderness that supports thousands of kinds of animals.

THYLACINE

Thylacines were wolflike marsupials with striped backs and powerful jaws. We know their appearance exactly, since the last one died in 1936. For tens of thousands of years they were the chief hunters on the island of Tasmania. But when the British settled this Australian island, they cut down much of the forest to raise sheep. Thylacines preyed on the sheep. So ranchers shot them. With little wilderness left to themselves, the thylacines were wiped out. Around the world, other island predators have suffered similar fates.

Thylacines may have played and hunted in packs as wolves do.

BUFFALO ARE BACK

Recent attempts to save some almost-extinct animals may be working. When Europeans first came to the American West, there were so many buffalo that passengers on the first train rides would shoot them from their windows just for fun. Hunters drove them to the brink of extinction in only one hundred years. But now the buffalo is back. Thousands of wild buffalo live on protected lands, and many more domesticated buffalo are bred on farms for their meat.

RIGHT NOW—THE HOLOCENE EXTINCTION

Right now we are in the middle of a giant extinction event. Animals are disappearing forever at one hundred to one thousand times nature's usual rate. Around the world, the dangers to animal life are great, especially in the tropical rain forests—a narrow belt of ten percent of the Earth's land that contains more than half of all living things. The rain forest is disappearing so fast that most of it may well be gone within the next fifty years. If the rain forest is destroyed, as many as three million kinds of animals, large and small, may go extinct with it.

Many people are working to save the rain forest and other endangered habitats. With our help, some animals have been rescued from the brink of extinction, among them the California condor, the black-footed ferret, the whooping crane, the buffalo, and the oryx. Saving the environments that support these and less visible but equally important creatures is a challenge for all humankind.

AUROCHS ▶

or-ahks
NAME: an ancient name, perhaps meaning "meadow ox"
TIME: 140,000 years ago until the 17th century
PLACE: central Europe
SIZE: 6 feet (1.8 m) high at the shoulder
This wild ox roamed the forests of central Europe. Forest clearing wiped the aurochs out by 1400 everywhere but in Poland. In 1627, the last wild aurochs died in a Polish forest. Domestic cattle probably descended from the aurochs.

◀ CAROLINA PARAKEET

kair-oh-lie-nuh **pair**-a-keet
NAME: for the early English colony of Carolina (later divided into North and South Carolina), where it first became known to Europeans
TIME: probably 5 million years ago until the early 20th century
PLACE: southeastern USA
SIZE: 4 inches (10 cm) long
Green- and yellow-headed with orange markings, this beautiful bird was a source of feathers for Indians and colonists. Common in the early 1800s, it was hunted into extinction by 1920.

GREAT AUK ▶

awk
NAME: from "alk," the Norwegian name for this bird and for its large size compared to other kinds of auks
TIME: until the mid-19th century
PLACE: shores of North America, Iceland, England, Scandinavia, Spain
SIZE: 2½ feet (75 cm) high
A clumsy, flightless bird resembling a penguin. A favorite source of oil for fishermen, it was wiped out by the mid-1800s.

▲ HEATH HEN

heeth hen
NAME: for the brushy open land, called a heath, where it lived, and because it was related to chickens
TIME: about 1 million years ago (or earlier) until the 19th century
PLACE: New England to the Southern Atlantic (USA)
SIZE: 10 inches (25 cm) long
The heath hen was a chunky prairie chicken. Males inflated orange sacs in their necks during courting. Once a common food source, by 1870 they were wiped out everywhere but in Martha's Vineyard, Massachusetts, where the last heath hen died in 1932.

▼ PORTUGUESE IBEX

por-chew-geez **ie**-beks
NAME: "goat" in Latin
TIME: from about 150,000 years ago until 1892
PLACE: Portugal and Spain
SIZE: 32 inches (80 cm) high at the shoulders
This horned mountain goat was hunted to extinction.

JAVAN TIGER ▶

jah-vuhn **tie**-guhr
NAME: for the island of
Java, where it lived
TIME: probably from about
100,000 years ago until 1972
PLACE: Java (Indonesia)
SIZE: 5 feet (1.5 m) long
(head and body)
This tiger was last sighted in
1972. It was the smallest of
all the modern forms of tiger.

◀ STELLER'S SEA COW

stel-uhrz **see kow**
NAME: for German naturalist Georg
Steller who discovered it in 1741
TIME: from 10 million years ago until
the mid-18th century
PLACE: Bering Straits, Arctic Ocean
SIZE: up to 30 feet (9 m) long
This 4-ton giant manatee-like animal
was eaten by sailors and killed off by
1768, soon after it was discovered.
It was the first sea mammal to be
driven to extinction by modern
humans.

▼ QUAGGA

kwawg-guh
NAME: local African name, from the
shrill barking sound they made
TIME: from about 200,000 years ago
until 1883
PLACE: South Africa
SIZE: 6.2 feet (2 m) long
Small herds of these animals were
once a common sight. But since they
ate the grass that settlers wanted
for their cattle, and because their
hides were useful, settlers killed
them. The last quagga died in a
zoo in Amsterdam in 1883.

COLUMBA JOUYI ▶

kuh-**luhm**-ba **joh**-ee-ie
NAME: "Jouy's dove," for P.L. Jouy, a man who
collected bird specimens in China and Japan
TIME: probably from about 100,000 years ago
until 1945
PLACE: Okinawa (Japan)
SIZE: 6 inches (15 cm) long
Also called the Okinawa pigeon, this bird tasted
good on an island with many hungry people.

GLOSSARY

ammonite A common type of cephalopod during the Carboniferous and Permian periods, they became extinct about 60 million years ago.

amphibian Carnivorous animal with moist skin that lays soft eggs in water and lives both in water and on land. They flourished during the Carboniferous and Perimian periods, and many survive to this day.

bird-hipped dinosaur See ornithischihan.

bivalve Any ocean-dwelling, shelled animal with two identical halves, such as the modern clam.

brachiopod Any ocean-dwelling, shelled animal with two halves of different sizes and shapes, having a beak at the shell hinge and a fleshy stalk. They were quite common during the Ordovician period, but are rare today.

creodont Any member of the group of the earliest carnivorous mammals to thrive, appearing about 65 million years ago. They had long tails, small brains, and came in all sizes.

crinoid Type of ocean animal that was anchored to the sea floor by a stalk. They were extremely common during the Carboniferous and Permian periods. Also called "sea lily."

cyanobacteria Some of the earliest organisms, these single-celled creatures gave off oxygen as waste.

cynodont Any of a group of small, meat-eating reptiles that thrived during the Triassic period. They may have had much in common with mammals, including body hair, a variety of teeth, and perhaps even warm-bloodedness.

diapsid Land animals that have two openings in each side of the back of their skulls. Modern diapsids include crocodiles, lizards, and birds.

dicynodont Any of several large, plant-eating animals common during the Triassic period that had upper jaws ending in beaks and two tusks. They used these snouts for cutting plants and, possibly, for digging underground shelters.

dinosaur Any of a group of animals that appeared during the Triassic period and disappeared at the end of the Cretaceous. They had specialized ankles and hips that allowed them to carry their bodies directly above their legs.

euryapsid An animal that has a single hole high on each side of its skull.

extinction The death of all members of a species.

fossil Remnant of an organism preserved in stone.

gastropod A class of mollusks that have heads, feet, and mantles that make protective shells.

human Any of a group of mammals with large brains who walk upright on two legs.

insect Any of a large group of animals with a hard, external, jointed skeleton and a three-part body.

lizard-hipped dinosaur   See saurischian.

lungfish   A fleshy fish with thick, rounded, scaly fins, heavy bones, and strong muscles. It is the only type of lobe-finned fish that survived the Devonian period and still exists today.

mammal   Any one of a group of warm-blooded animals with hair-covered bodies. Most give birth to live young. All nurse their young.

millipede   An anthropod with many legs, it was among the first anthropods to conquer land.

mosasaur   Any one of a group of large, fish-eating, sea-dwelling reptiles that thrived from the Triassic period to the Cretaceous period.

oreodont   Any of a large group of piglike mammals that lived during the Pleistocene period.

ornithischian   One of two classifications of dinosaurs (the other is saurischian). The difference is in the structure of the hips. Ornithischians had pubic bones that pointed backward, like a bird's.

plesiosaur   A type of sea reptile with a short tail, legs like paddles, and a very long neck. Plesiosaurs lived during the Triassic and Jurassic periods.

pliosaur   The largest of the plesiosaurs, they were 40 feet (12 m) long.

primate   An animal possessing a large brain, short jaws, forward-facing eyes, and five toes and fingers. Humans are primates, and so are chimpanzees and gorillas.

pterosaur   One of a group of winged reptiles that lived near the water. They had leathery skin instead of feathers and were the first vertebrates to fly. They lived during the time of the dinosaurs.

reptile   A group of scaly-skinned, cold-blooded land animals that lay eggs with hard shells. They were the first animals with backbones to live and reproduce on land.

saurischian   One of two classifications of dinosaurs (the other is ornithischian). The difference is in the structure of the hips. Saurischians (including all carnivorous dinosaurs) had public bones that pointed down, like those of lizards.

sauropod   A giant dinosaur that lived during the Jurassic period. They ate plants, walked on four legs, and could be as large as 120 feet (36 m) long, though they had small heads.

shark   A type of fish that appeared during the Silurian and Devonian periods and survives to this day. Sharks have skeletons made of cartilage, tiny scales, and very sharp teeth.

stromatolite   Bits of sediment left by groups of primitive microscopic organisms, they are one of the earliest records of life on earth.

synapsid   Any one of a group of land animals that lived during the Carboniferous and Permian periods. They had a single opening on each side of their skulls, and most ate meat.

thecodont   A giant, four-legged early reptile that lived during the Triassic period. They were ancestors of dinosaurs and of the crocodile.

titanotheres   A group of piglike mammals that, though small in the early part of the Pleistocene period, grew quite large by the middle of the period. They had disappeared by the close of the Pleistocene.

Vendian animals   Disk-shaped organisms from the Precambrian period, they are some of the oldest known ancestors of life on earth.

INDEX

RESOURCES

BOOKS

The Complete Idiot's Guide to Dinosaurs by George McGhee and Jay Stevenson, Alpha Books, 1998.

Dinosaur Society Dinosaur Encyclopedia by Don Lessem and Donald Glut, Random House, 1993. A current and complete dictionary of dinosaurs. Available from: Dinosaur Productions, P.O. Box 461, Newton Center, MA 02459.

Dinosaur Worlds by Don Lessem, Boyd's Mills Press, 1997.

Extinction is Forever by Donald Silver, Julian Messner Publishing, 1996.

Eyewitness Handbooks: *Fossils* by Cyril Walker and David Ward, Dorling Kindersley, 1992.

Eyewitness Visual Dictionary of Prehistoric Life, Dorling Kindersley, 1995.

A Field Guide to Prehistoric Life by David Lambert and the Diagram Group, Facts on File, 1994.

Fossils of the Burgess Shale by Derek Briggs, Douglas Erwin, and Frederick Collier, Smithsonian Institution Press, 1995.

I Can Read About Fossils by John Howard, Troll, 1997.

Simon and Schuster's Field Guide to Fossils by Paolo Arduini and Giorgio Teruzzi, Simon and Schuster, 1987.

CD-ROMs:

Grolier's Prehistoria: The Multimedia Who's Who of Prehistoric Life, 1994.

Microsoft Dinosaurs, 1993.

FOSSIL CASTS

To obtain information, write to:
Dinosaur Productions
P.O. Box 461
Newton Center, MA 02459

PALEONTOLOGICAL EXPEDITIONS

Museum of the Rockies
Paleontology Field Program
600 W. Kagy Boulevard
Bozeman, MT 59717
406-994-6618

Dinosaur Discovery Expeditions
550 Jurassic Court
Fruita, CO 81521
800-344-3466

Earthwatch
680 Mt. Auburn Street
Watertown, MA 02472
617-926-8200

VIDEO TAPE

Life in the Rocks, Turner Broadcasting, Atlanta, GA, 1995.

WEBSITES

For the University of California at Berkeley Museum of Paleontology, visit: *www.ucmp.berkeley.edu*

For fun and facts on dinosaurs for kids and grown-ups, visit: *www.dinodon.com*

For the Chicago Field Museum of Natural History, visit: *www.fmnh.org*